A First Baking Book

SHEEP can't BAKE

But YOU can!

Teach yourself how to bake with Sheep and his friends!

Noodle Juice Ltd
www.noodle-juice.com
Stonesfield House, Stanwell Lane,
Great Bourton, Oxfordshire, OX17 1QS

First published in Great Britain 2023
Copyright © Noodle Juice Ltd 2023
Text by Noodle Juice 2022

Illustrations by Mr Griff 2022
Photography by Tina Knowles

ISBN: 9781915613141
3 5 7 9 10 8 6 4 2

FSC
www.fsc.org
MIX
Paper | Supporting
responsible forestry
FSC® C005748

This book is made from
FSC®-certified paper.
By choosing this book,
you help to take care of
the world's forests.
Learn more: www.fsc.org.

Sheep Can't Bake, but YOU can!

CONTENTS

Let's get baking!

Welcome to Sheep Can't Bake

This fantastic book will teach you eight core baking skills and how to apply each skill to make delicious recipes. By the end of the book, you – and hopefully Sheep – will be able to bake over 50 wonderful cakes, bakes, cookies, pies, breads and muffins.

At every stage, our cast of friendly animals will be advising you (or not!) on how to make the best cakes and bakes!

There are also handy baking tips and techniques (see pages 108–110), as well as fascinating facts about the ingredients used in the recipes and the origins of some of your favourite treats.

> Remember, all the different techniques you need for baking are explained in the core recipes at the beginning of each section.

Meet the team

PIG

The expert baker. Pig is full of advice to make sure you bake the best cakes you can.

> I trained under Gordon Hamsay, you know!

RABBIT

In charge of health and safety. Rabbit will remind you to be careful when using sharp knives or the oven. If he says you should ask a grown-up to help, then make sure you do!

GROWN-UP'S HELP NEEDED!

SHEEP

Has a lot to learn!

> But I can bake, really I can! I just need a bit more practice.

Food allergies

Some people have food allergies or intolerances. Recipes that contain nuts are clearly marked. There is a dairy-free and gluten-free section with some delicious recipes too (see pages 94–107).

Each recipe clearly states if it contains wheat, gluten, dairy products, egg or nuts.

WARNING!
FOOD ALLERGIES

I think I make a great storage container myself!

Food storage

You may need to store what you've baked – so make sure you have cake tins or plastic storage containers to hand to keep your delicious cakes fresh.

Essential Equipment

The recipes in this book can be made with the utensils shown below, as well as the most amazing tools of all, your hands! Always check that you have what you need to hand before starting to bake.

 When you see this symbol, you can use an electric hand mixer to make your life a little easier!

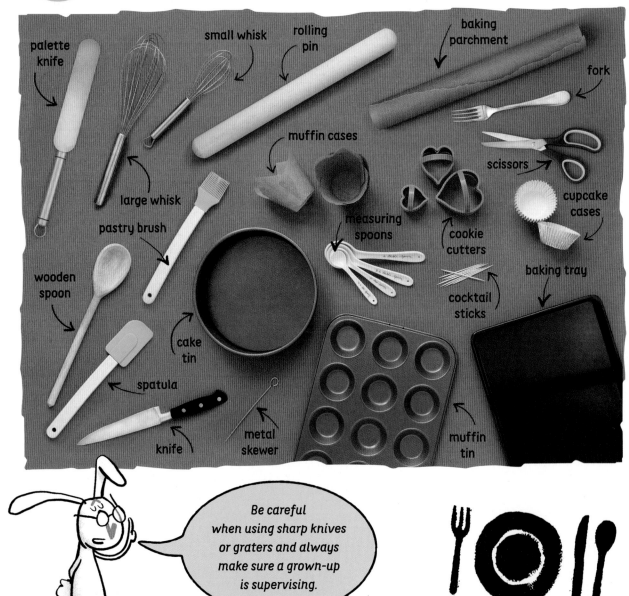

palette knife

small whisk

rolling pin

baking parchment

fork

large whisk

muffin cases

scissors

cupcake cases

pastry brush

measuring spoons

cookie cutters

baking tray

wooden spoon

cocktail sticks

cake tin

spatula

knife

metal skewer

muffin tin

Be careful when using sharp knives or graters and always make sure a grown-up is supervising.

Baking tins and trays

Each recipe recommends a particular cake tin or baking tray to use. If you don't have the same-sized tins, the recipes will still taste the same but your cakes might look a bit different to the photographs and you may need to adjust the cooking time. The list below tells you what sizes are used throughout the book!

20cm-diameter loose-bottom cake tin
23cm-diameter loose-bottom tart tin
20cm-diameter pie dish
23cm x 23cm brownie tin
24cm x 33cm baking tray
12-hole muffin tin
12-hole bun tin
8cm x 21cm loaf tin
24cm x 33cm roasting tin

It's a good idea to wear an apron to keep your clothes clean while baking.

mixing bowl

oven gloves

grater

measuring jug

sieve

baking beans

wire rack

saucepan

juicer

frying pan

I suppose I could always put myself through on a woollen cycle!

Essential Ingredients

Here are most of the ingredients you will need to make the recipes in the book. There are lots of different types of flours and sugars. You can mix up ingredients to create new flavours. Why not experiment with flavours you like?

Polenta and ground almonds are good substitutes for flour, when you need to make cakes that are gluten-free.

dried yeast

cinnamon

plain flour

desiccated coconut

self-raising flour

baking powder

bicarbonate of soda

soft light brown sugar

icing sugar

golden caster sugar

polenta

ground almonds

strong bread flour

salt

dried oregano

ginger

soft dark brown sugar

cocoa powder

rolled oats

butter

golden syrup

buttermilk

yoghurt

crunchy peanut butter

vanilla essence

cream cheese

honey

lemon curd

sour cream

maple syrup

olive oil

apricot jam

egg

condensed milk

white wine vinegar

milk

raspberry jam

double cream

vegetable oil

Flour

- **Plain flour** is the most versatile, and is used in biscuits and pastry.

- **Self-raising flour** is plain flour that includes a raising agent, such as baking powder. It's great for cakes and traybakes.

- **Strong flour** is used for making bread dough, as it contains more gluten, which makes the dough stretchy.

The three flours can be white, wholemeal or granary, depending on how much of the grain is included in the flour. The browner the flour, the more husk is present and the more fibre the flour contains.

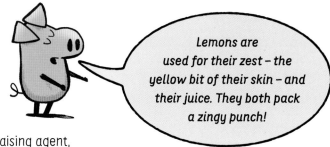

Lemons are used for their zest – the yellow bit of their skin – and their juice. They both pack a zingy punch!

lemon, lime, raisins, strawberries, raspberries, orange, garlic, dates, plum tomato, blueberries, pineapple, banana, apple, coconut, glacé cherries, carrots, onion

WARNING! FOOD ALLERGIES

If you are baking for your friends, find out if they have any allergies first – nuts can be especially tricky!

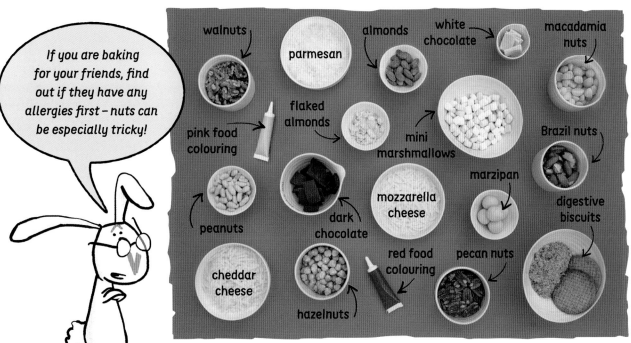

walnuts, parmesan, almonds, white chocolate, macadamia nuts, flaked almonds, mini marshmallows, Brazil nuts, pink food colouring, marzipan, digestive biscuits, peanuts, dark chocolate, mozzarella cheese, cheddar cheese, hazelnuts, red food colouring, pecan nuts

9

Getting Started

Baking is often called a science rather than an art. This is because it is important to use the right amount of each ingredient – like in a science experiment – otherwise the recipe might not work.

Follow the recipe

Before you start baking, read the recipe carefully to make sure you understand what you need to do. Assemble all the ingredients and equipment before you begin, so that you have everything ready.

Weighing and measuring

It's a good idea to practise using your weighing scales. Scales help you to measure the right amount of each ingredient. Most electronic ones let you go back to zero once you have put your measuring bowl on them, so you only weigh what you need, without having to do any maths!

Using a microwave

GROWN-UP'S HELP NEEDED!

Always make sure you have a grown-up present and never, ever put anything metal into the microwave. Remember to use oven gloves when getting food in and out too.

Microwaves are really useful, but do need treating with respect.

Eggs

All recipes have been made using medium-sized eggs.

Baking parchment

Sometimes called greaseproof paper, baking parchment is your friend. It lines cake tins and baking trays, so that your cakes and biscuits don't get stuck. Make sure you have plenty to hand before you start to bake!

Butter

Most recipes ask for 'butter, softened'. The best way to make sure the butter is soft is to take it out of the fridge at least an hour before you want to use it. That way, it is much easier to mix. Some recipes, such as pastry, need cold butter which can be used straight from the fridge. All butter used in these recipes is unsalted.

It's best to break up the butter into smaller pieces before adding it to the mixing bowl to make it easier to mix with the other ingredients.

GROWN-UP'S HELP NEEDED!

Oven

A lot of the recipes need an oven. Always ask a grown-up to help you turn the oven on to the correct temperature. Different ovens heat up at different speeds, so some cakes might need a bit longer in the oven than the recipe suggests, or a bit less.

The temperatures listed in the book are for a fan oven, so if you are using an oven without a fan, increase the temperature by 20°C or 35°F.

Should have been five hours less, I think! That's going to need a LOT of icing...

Once your cake is in the oven, it's best not to open the door too often. When you need to check if a cake is cooked, try to do it as quickly as you can!

Just remember to wear your oven gloves!

CORE BAKING SKILL
#1 Cakes and Cupcakes

A classic sponge cake filled with buttercream and jam is the foundation for baking cakes. Once you know how to make it, you will be surprised at how many different kinds of cupcakes and layer cakes you'll be able to bake, simply by adding different flavours or ingredients or toppings.

Victoria Sponge Cake

Cake ingredients

225g butter, softened
225g caster sugar
4 eggs
225g self-raising flour
1 teaspoon baking powder
1 tablespoon milk (optional)

For the icing

50g butter, softened
100g icing sugar
4 tablespoons raspberry jam

For decoration

2 tablespoons icing sugar

You will need 2 loose-bottom cake tins, 20cm in diameter.

ALLERGIES

Wheat, gluten, dairy, eggs

The 'creaming' technique adds air to the cake mix. Make sure that the butter and sugar are mixed together really well, so the mix looks light and creamy. It needs a lot of elbow grease!

Method 1

1 Heat the oven to 160°C / 350°F or gas mark 4. Grease and line both sandwich tins.

For instructions on how to easily grease and line your cake tins, turn to page 108.

2 Using a wooden spoon, cream the butter and sugar together in a large bowl until light and fluffy.

3 Break the eggs into another bowl and whisk together with a fork. Make sure you don't include any egg shell!

4 Sieve the flour and baking powder into another mixing bowl.

5 Add a quarter of the beaten egg and a quarter of the flour mixture to the butter and sugar bowl, and mix well with a wooden spoon. Repeat three more times until all the eggs and flour have been mixed in. If the mixture is a bit stiff and hard to stir, add the milk and mix again.

6 Split the mixture between the two cake tins, using a spatula to scrape out all the cake mix. Spread the mixture flat in the tins and add a slight dip to the centre.

7 Put the cakes in the oven and bake for 20 minutes. When the time is up, press a cake with your finger to see if it springs back. If not, leave in the oven for another 5 minutes.

This will help to keep the cake tops flat when they bake in the oven.

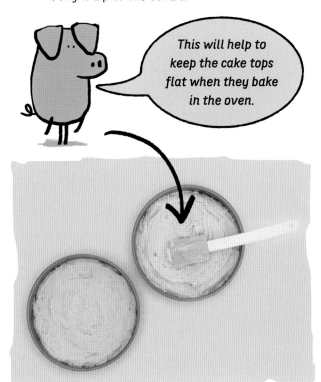

There are several ways to check whether your cake is cooked. You can insert a metal skewer and if it is clean when you pull it out, the cake is cooked. Another good sign is if the cake has come away from the sides of the tin slightly.

GROWN-UP'S HELP NEEDED!

8 When the cakes are cooked, leave them in their tins for 5 minutes to stand, and then turn them out on a wire rack to cool further.

See page 109 for a great tip on how to take your cakes out of their tins.

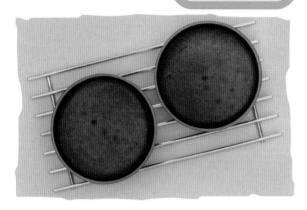

9 To make the icing, sieve the icing sugar into a bowl, add the butter and then cream together until smooth.

That's not 'gently', Sheep!

10 Look at your two cakes. Is one more level than the other? Choose the best one to be on the top. Take the cake you want on the bottom and put it on a plate, flat side up, remembering to remove the baking parchment. Spread the buttercream icing all over the flat surface with a spatula. Using the back of a spoon, spread your jam on top.

Top Tip

If your jam is too solid to spread easily, put it in a bowl and ask a grown-up to heat it up in the microwave for 15 seconds.

You can use any jam you like if you don't have raspberry. We appear to have run out for some reason...

14

11 Place your remaining cake on top of the jam (minus the baking parchment) flat side down, and sprinkle the remaining icing sugar through a sieve on to the cake.

You can also use a mixer for the icing, but be very careful as icing sugar can go everywhere! You could cover your mixer with a clean tea towel to keep the icing sugar contained.

Method 2

1 If you do have either a electric hand mixer or a stand mixer, it takes much less time to make the cake. Simply put all the cake ingredients, except the milk, into the mixing bowl (making sure that the butter is soft) and mix together for 2 or 3 minutes.

2 If the cake mix is very stiff, then add the milk and mix again.

3 Now follow Method 1 from step 6.

Butterfly Cupcakes

Now you know how to make a basic sponge cake, it is easy to turn the mixture into gorgeous butterfly cupcakes to share with your friends. You can add pretty decorations or icing sugar to make them extra appealing. These cakes are called butterfly cupcakes because of the shape of the sponge wings!

Cupcake ingredients
150g butter, softened
150g caster sugar
3 eggs
150g self-raising flour
½ tablespoon milk (optional)

For the icing
75g butter, softened
150g icing sugar

For decoration
1 tablespoon icing sugar
Silver balls or sprinkles

You will need a 12-hole muffin tin and 12 paper cupcake cases.

ALLERGIES
Wheat, gluten, dairy, eggs

I don't see why we have to eat butterflies – wouldn't they be crunchy?

Method

1 Heat the oven to 160°C / 350°F or gas mark 4.

Don't forget to ask a grown-up's permission!

2 Cream the butter and sugar together in a bowl until light and fluffy. Beat the eggs in a separate bowl. Add small amounts of egg to the butter and sugar mixture, alternating with small amounts of flour until they are all mixed together. Add the milk if the mixture is a bit stiff.

3 Put a paper case into each hole of the muffin tin and use two teaspoons to fill the paper cases almost to the top.

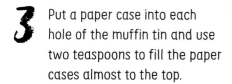

Use one teaspoon to push the cake mix off the other spoon into the paper cases.

4 Bake the cakes in the oven for 16–18 minutes. Once out of the oven, leave in the tin for 5 minutes and then place on a wire rack to cool.

5 To make the filling, sieve the icing sugar into a bowl, add the butter and then cream together until smooth.

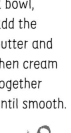

6 To assemble the cupcakes, use a sharp knife at an angle to cut a circle from the top of each cake. Then cut the circle in half to make wings.

Make sure you leave a border of cake between the case and the edge of the hole!

7 Fill each hole with icing and then place two cake 'wings' gently on to the buttercream, leaving a small gap in the middle for decorations.

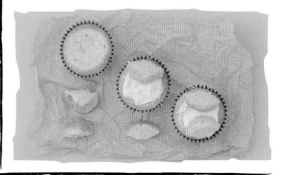

8 Take the silver balls or sprinkles and carefully place down the centre of the 'wings' to create the body of the butterfly. Finally, take a small sieve and tip in a teaspoon of icing sugar. Tap the sieve gently to lightly dust the cupcakes with icing sugar.

My cakes don't want to fly. Maybe they're not light enough?

They're not real wings, silly!

17

Red Velvet Cupcakes

Red velvet cupcakes are mini versions of the original red velvet cake made famous by New York hotel, the Waldorf Astoria. A delicious chocolate cake is made magical with red food colouring and cream cheese icing.

During World War II, bakers used beetroot juices to make their cakes red.

I don't think beetroot and I should mix!

Cupcake ingredients

150g plain flour
25g cocoa powder
1 teaspoon bicarbonate of soda
50g butter, softened
150g caster sugar
1 egg, beaten
1 teaspoon vanilla extract
100ml buttermilk
50ml vegetable oil
1 teaspoon white wine vinegar
1 tablespoon red food colouring

For the cream cheese icing

75g butter, softened
165g icing sugar
75g full-fat cream cheese

For decoration

Pretty cake decorations

You will need 12 paper cupcake cases and a 12-hole muffin tin, a piping bag and star-shaped nozzle (optional).

ALLERGIES
Wheat, gluten, dairy, eggs

Method

1 Heat the oven to 160°C / 350°F or gas mark 4. Line a muffin tin with cupcake cases.

2 Sieve the flour, cocoa and bicarbonate of soda into a bowl.

Cocoa powder can be used to make hot chocolate, but drinking chocolate can't be used as cocoa powder. Check that you have the right one.

3 Using a wooden spoon, cream the butter and sugar together in a large bowl until light and fluffy. Add the egg, vanilla extract, buttermilk, vegetable oil and vinegar, and mix well with a whisk.

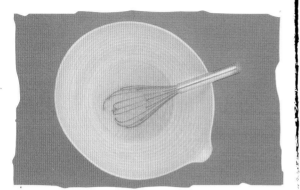

4 Add a quarter of the flour and cocoa mixture to the bowl and mix well. Repeat three times, until all the flour and cocoa has been mixed in, and then add the food colouring.

I am getting better at this, honest!

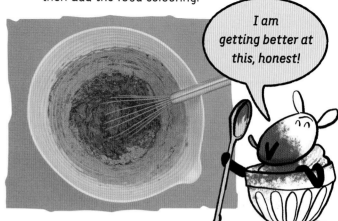

5 Using two teaspoons, share the mixture between the 12 cupcake cases. Try to make sure they are equal sizes so they cook evenly. Bake in the oven for 15 minutes. Leave to cool completely before icing.

6 For the cream cheese icing, gently mix the icing sugar and butter together in a bowl until pale and fluffy. Add the cream cheese, and mix well.

Make sure your cream cheese is room temperature – you might need to stir it to loosen before adding.

7 To ice the cupcakes, you can use a teaspoon or you can pipe it using a star-shaped nozzle. (See page 110 for tips on piping.)

8 Finally, add your decorations.

Pineapple Upside-down Cake

I'm not sure this is going to work! Am I doing it right?

Upside-down cakes are exactly as they sound. They are baked in the oven and then turned upside down to reveal a delicious fruit topping. Pineapple upside-down cake is popular in the USA and Brazil, while the French version is made with apples and pastry, and called a *tarte tatin.*

Fun Facts

Pineapples are actually berries.

Pineapples are a tropical fruit.

Pineapple plants produce just one pineapple a season.

I love pineapple on pizza!

Eww! No thanks!

Cake ingredients

150g butter, softened
150g soft light brown sugar
1 teaspoon vanilla extract
3 eggs
150g self-raising flour

For the fruit topping

50g butter, softened
50g soft light brown sugar
7 tinned pineapple rings in syrup
7 glacé cherries

You will need 1 cake tin, 20cm in diameter.

ALLERGIES

Wheat, gluten, dairy, eggs

Method

1 Heat the oven to 160°C / 350°F or gas mark 4. Grease and line the cake tin. Drain the pineapple slices, keeping the syrup from the tin.

Be careful when opening the tin. The lid can be sharp!

2 Using a wooden spoon, cream the butter and sugar together in a large bowl until light and fluffy. Break the eggs into another bowl and whisk together with a fork. Add the vanilla extract and two tablespoons of pineapple syrup to the egg mixture.

3 Sieve the flour into a different mixing bowl. Add half of the beaten egg and half of the flour to the butter and sugar bowl. Mix with the wooden spoon. Repeat once more until all the eggs and flour have been mixed in.

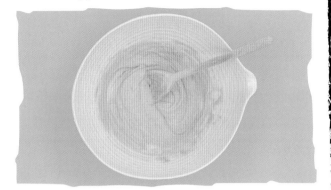

4 Next, prepare your topping. Cream together the butter and sugar and spread over the base of the cake tin. Make sure you fill it a quarter of the way up the sides.

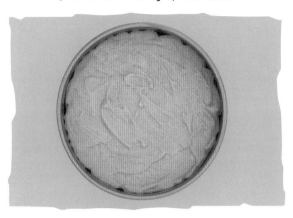

5 Arrange your pineapple slices and glacé cherries on the butter and sugar mix, then spread the cake mix on top of the pineapple.

Don't forget to add a dip in the middle so the cake top is flat when baked.

6 Bake in the oven for 35 minutes. When the cake is cooked, remove from the oven and leave to stand for 5 minutes. Tip the cake out on to a plate, so the beautiful pineapple rings are now on top. Serve with ice cream or cream.

Lemon Drizzle Cake

Lemon drizzle cake relies on fresh lemon juice and sugar for its moist texture and crunchy top. This cake is baked in a loaf tin and is perfect for a mid-afternoon snack.

Fun Facts

Lemons are a great source of Vitamin C.

Lemons were introduced into Europe around 1000CE.

Lemons can conduct electricity.

Wow, 1000CE - that's some really old lemons! Aren't they mouldy by now?

Cake ingredients

225g butter, softened
225g caster sugar
225g self-raising flour
1 teaspoon baking powder
4 eggs, beaten
1 large lemon, zested

For the drizzle

1½ lemons, juiced
85g granulated sugar

You will need a loaf tin, 8cm x 21cm.

ALLERGIES

Wheat, gluten, dairy, eggs

It says zest, not vest! Lemon zest is the thin yellow bit of the lemon rind.

But mind your fingers! Graters can be sharp!

Method

1 Heat the oven to 160°C / 350°F or gas mark 4. Line the loaf tin with baking parchment – see page 108 for tips on how to do this.

2 Use the small hole side on a grater to grate the yellow zest from the lemon rind, and put in a bowl. Cut the lemon in half and squeeze out the lemon juice using a juicer. You will need one and a half lemons. Wrap up the other half and keep it in the fridge for another day.

3 Using a wooden spoon, cream the butter and sugar together in a large bowl until light and fluffy. Sieve the flour and baking powder together in a bowl. Mix the eggs and flour with the butter and sugar in stages. Add the lemon zest and stir.

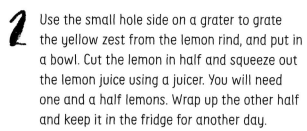

What's a juicer?

I don't think we'll be using that!

4 Tip the mixture into the lined loaf tin and use the spatula to put a slight dip in the centre. Bake in the oven for 45 minutes. Test with a metal skewer to see if it is cooked.

5 While the cake is cooking, put the lemon juice and granulated sugar in a jug and stir to make a syrup.

6 Once the cake is cooked, take it out of the oven and prick it all over with a skewer or a fork. Slowly pour the lemon syrup over the cake so it can sink in, leaving the sugar to form a lovely crunchy top. Leave in the tin until completely cold before turning out.

I can guarantee this won't hang around for long!

Be careful – the cake tin will be very hot.

Chocolate Gâteau

Everyone loves chocolate cake. This recipe is really chocolatey and uses cocoa powder to give the cake its flavour. It is filled with rich chocolate buttercream and decorated with chocolate shavings for that extra special touch. (See page 110 for instructions.)

We use the classic sponge method to make the chocolate gâteau too. The cocoa makes the cake super chocolatey! Yummy!

What's a gâteau?

The French word for cake.

Ooooh fancy!

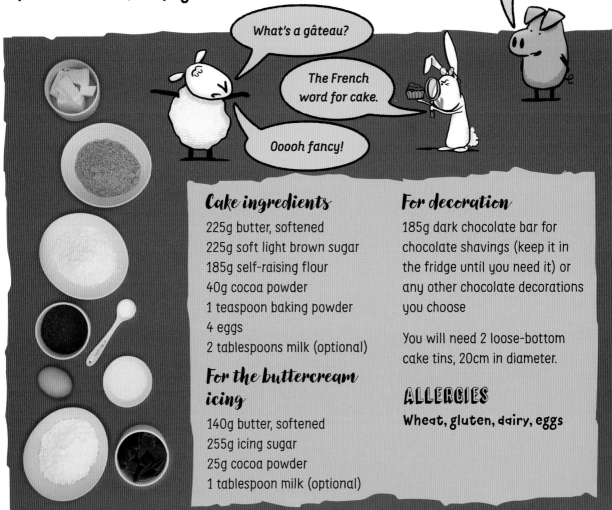

Cake ingredients

225g butter, softened
225g soft light brown sugar
185g self-raising flour
40g cocoa powder
1 teaspoon baking powder
4 eggs
2 tablespoons milk (optional)

For the buttercream icing

140g butter, softened
255g icing sugar
25g cocoa powder
1 tablespoon milk (optional)

For decoration

185g dark chocolate bar for chocolate shavings (keep it in the fridge until you need it) or any other chocolate decorations you choose

You will need 2 loose-bottom cake tins, 20cm in diameter.

ALLERGIES
Wheat, gluten, dairy, eggs

Method

1 Heat the oven to 160°C / 350°F or gas mark 4. Grease and line both cake tins.

2 Using a wooden spoon, cream the butter and sugar together in a large bowl until light and fluffy. Break the eggs into another bowl and whisk together with a fork.

3 Sieve the flour, cocoa powder and baking powder into a different mixing bowl.

This is where we add the cocoa and use slightly less flour.

4 Add a quarter of the beaten egg and a quarter of the flour mixture to the butter and sugar bowl, and mix well with the wooden spoon. Repeat three times until all the eggs and flour have been mixed in. You may need to add the milk at this stage if the cake mix is too stiff.

I really am getting better at this, don't you think?

5 Split the mixture between the two cake tins, using a spatula to scrape out all the cake mix. Spread the mixture flat in the tins and make slight dips in the centres.

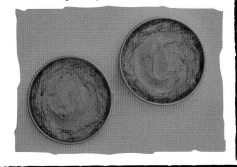

6 Put the cakes in the oven and bake for 20 minutes. When the cakes are cooked, take them out and leave them in their tins to stand for 5 minutes. Then, turn them out on a wire rack to cool further.

7 Mix the icing sugar and the remaining cocoa powder and butter together in bowl until smooth. Use milk to loosen the icing if it is too stiff to spread easily.

8 Sandwich the two layers together using a third of the buttercream. Spread the rest of the icing on the top and sides as smoothly as you can. It helps to turn the plate around as you do so. Sprinkle chocolate shavings on top.

Strawberry Birthday Layer Cake

Can it be my birthday every day, please?

This impressive looking cake is actually really easy to make. You just need patience! The delicious combination of strawberries and vanilla icing makes it a lovely summery cake, and doesn't have to be just for birthdays. Any celebration will do!

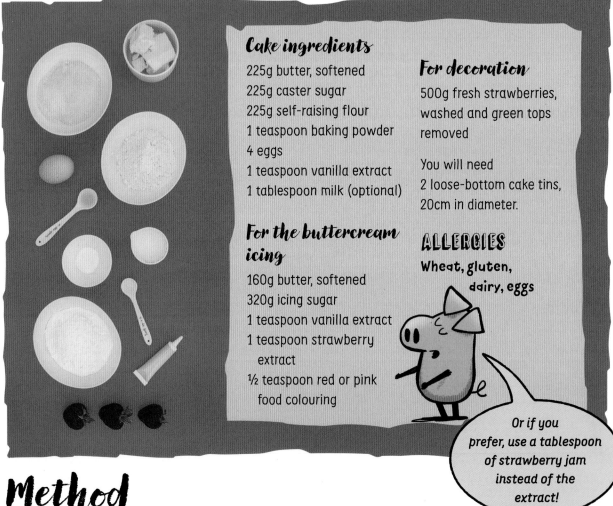

Cake ingredients

225g butter, softened
225g caster sugar
225g self-raising flour
1 teaspoon baking powder
4 eggs
1 teaspoon vanilla extract
1 tablespoon milk (optional)

For the buttercream icing

160g butter, softened
320g icing sugar
1 teaspoon vanilla extract
1 teaspoon strawberry
   extract
½ teaspoon red or pink
   food colouring

For decoration

500g fresh strawberries, washed and green tops removed

You will need
2 loose-bottom cake tins, 20cm in diameter.

ALLERGIES
Wheat, gluten, dairy, eggs

Or if you prefer, use a tablespoon of strawberry jam instead of the extract!

Method

1 Heat the oven to 160°C / 350°F or gas mark 4. Grease and line both cake tins.

2 Using a wooden spoon, cream the butter and sugar together in a large bowl until light and fluffy. Break the eggs into another bowl with the vanilla extract and whisk together with a fork. Sieve the flour and the baking powder into a different bowl.

3 Add a quarter of the beaten egg and a quarter of the flour mixture to the butter and sugar bowl. Mix well with the wooden spoon. Repeat three times, until all the eggs and flour have been mixed in. If the mixture is a bit stiff and hard to stir, add the milk and mix again.

4 Split the mixture between the two cake tins, using a spatula to scrape out all the cake mix. Spread the mixture flat in the tins and put a slight dip in the centre of each.

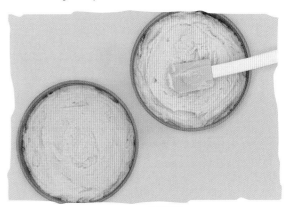

5 Put the cakes in the oven and bake for 20 minutes. When the cakes are cooked, leave them in their tins to cool for 5 minutes, and then turn them out on a wire rack.

If you've been working through the recipes in order, this should seem very familiar now.

6 Once cool, carefully cut each cake in half to make four layers of sponge cake. The best way to do this is to take a serrated knife in one hand. Holding your other palm on top of the cake, gently saw horizontally through the cake.

You should ask a grown-up to help here!

7 For the filling, there are two flavours of buttercream icing. Cream together all the butter and icing sugar until smooth. Divide the buttercream into two. One portion should weigh 330g and the other should weigh 150g.

There's a lot of icing to make, so make sure that your butter is really soft.

8 Add the strawberry extract (or jam) and the food colouring to the smaller bowl of buttercream and mix. This icing is for layers one and three.

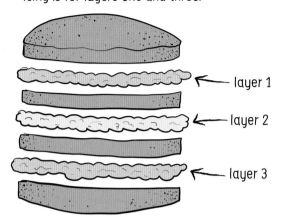

layer 1
layer 2
layer 3

9 Add the vanilla essence to the larger amount of icing and mix. This icing is for the middle layer, and the top and sides of the cake.

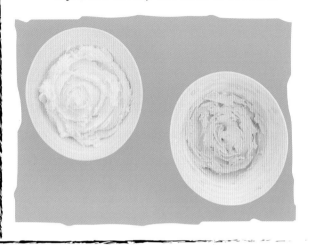

10 To assemble the cake, take one base layer (all layers should be cut-side down) and spread half the strawberry icing on top. Place another layer of cake on top. Follow with a third of the vanilla icing, then another layer of cake. Use the rest of the strawberry icing on this layer. Place the top layer on the cake. Use the rest of the vanilla icing to cover the top and sides of the cake.

Icing the sides of the cake can be tricky. Use a palette knife to spread the icing, and keep turning the cake in front of you. Once all the icing is on the cake, dip your palette knife in warm water, then dry it, before using to smooth the icing.

Like this?

11 To finish the cake, carefully cut the strawberries into slices vertically (from top to bottom of the strawberry). If they are juicy, dry the strawberries with some kitchen paper. Then press the strawberry slices into the sides of the cake in rows all around.

My turn at last! Be careful with the sharp knife and make sure a grown-up is nearby!

11 You can either leave the top plain, put a few strawberries in the middle or cover the whole surface – it's up to you! Eat immediately or keep in the fridge until needed.

Fun Facts

The average strawberry has 200 seeds.

Ancient Romans used strawberries as medicine to treat everything from depression to sore throats.

Strawberries are members of the rose family.

Happy birthday to me! Happy birthday to me! Happy birthday, dear Sheep...

CORE BAKING SKILL
#2 Traybakes

That's not what we use the tray for!

Traybakes are a great way to share your favourite cakes with friends. Once cooked in a tray, the cake can be cut into slices or squares. The core recipe is a chocolate brownie, but in this section, there are flapjacks, apple slices and even a no-bake rocky road. All are perfect for picnics, sharing with friends or school fundraisers.

Brownies
Ingredients

185g dark chocolate
185g butter, cut into cubes
250g caster sugar
3 eggs
2 teaspoons vanilla extract
150g walnuts or pecans (optional)
110g plain flour
½ teaspoon salt

You will need a square brownie tin, 23cm x 23cm.

Makes 9 brownies.

ALLERGIES
Wheat, gluten, dairy, eggs, nuts

Method

1 Heat the oven to 160°C / 350°F or gas mark 4. Grease and line your brownie tin with greaseproof paper, both sides and bottom (see page 108).

2 Melt the chocolate and butter in a bain-marie, stirring gently (see page 110 for instructions), or in the microwave. Remove from the heat.

Don't forget to use your oven gloves! The bowl will be hot.

30

3 In a large mixing bowl, beat together the sugar, eggs and vanilla extract using a whisk.

4 To chop the nuts, place them onto a chopping board and cut them into small pieces.

You will need to use a sharp knife to do this. Put your chopping board on a tea towel, so it doesn't slide around on your work surface.

5 Once the chocolate and butter mixture has cooled slightly, use a spatula to scrape it into the eggs and sugar mix and stir. Add the flour, salt and nuts and stir again, until all the flour has been mixed in.

6 Scrape the mixture into the lined baking tin, making sure you fill all the corners, and bake in the oven for 25 minutes.

Brownies are supposed to be squidgy in the middle, so the methods for checking a cake is cooked won't work here. When ready, the top should be light-brown and crispy, and the middle dark and gooey.

7 Remove from the oven and allow to cool in the tin. Then take the brownie traybake out of the tin, remove the parchment and cut into equal squares.

Blondies

A delicious variation of a brownie uses white chocolate instead of dark chocolate, and replaces walnuts or pecans with macadamia nuts, to make blondies. White chocolate contains more sugar and cocoa butter than dark chocolate, so the recipe is slightly different.

Ingredients

185g white chocolate
100g butter
250g soft light brown sugar
3 eggs
2 teaspoons vanilla extract
225g plain flour
½ teaspoon salt
150g macadamia nuts (optional)

Makes 9 blondies.

You will need a square brownie tin 23cm x 23cm.

ALLERGIES
Wheat, gluten, dairy, eggs, nuts

Method

1 Heat the oven to 150°C / 325°F or gas mark 3. Grease and line your brownie tin with greaseproof paper, both sides and bottom.

2 Melt the white chocolate and butter in a bain-marie or microwave. Remove from the heat.

White chocolate only contains cocoa butter, and none of the cocoa solids which would make it chocolate coloured!

What chocolate? I can't see any chocolate...

3 In a large mixing bowl, beat together the sugar, eggs and vanilla extract. Add the cooled chocolate mixture, the flour, salt and nuts and stir again.

4 Scrape into the brownie tin, and bake in the oven for 35 minutes. It will be cooked when the top has become nice and crispy.

I don't know which to choose. I shall just have to try one of each!

Flapjacks

Flapjacks are quick and easy to make.

A traditional flapjack is made from oats, butter, golden syrup and sugar, and baked in a tray. They can also be called oat bars, muesli bars or granola bars. If you want to make your flapjacks healthier, add 75g of dried fruit and nuts, or seeds, to the recipe.

Easy for you maybe... Golden syrup is sticky!

Sometimes rolled oats are called 'old-fashioned' or 'porridge'. For this recipe, don't use any oats called 'quick'!

Flapjack ingredients
100g soft light brown sugar
150g butter
100g golden syrup
300g rolled oats

You will need a square brownie tin, 23cm x 23cm.

Makes 9 flapjacks.

ALLERGIES
Dairy

Make sure you have asked a grown-up!

Method

1 Heat the oven to 170°C / 375°F or gas mark 5. Grease and line the brownie tin, including the sides.

2 Take a large pan and melt the sugar, butter and golden syrup together on a low heat until all the sugar has dissolved. This could take 5–10 minutes. Stir occasionally.

3 Remove the pan from the heat and add the rolled oats, stirring until all the oats are coated in the buttery mixture. If you are using fruit and nuts, add them here.

4 Tip the mixture into the brownie tin and press firmly into the edges, flattening to a smooth, level surface. Place in the oven and cook for 25 minutes until golden brown.

You can add all sorts of flavours and ingredients to make your basic flapjack even more delicious. Why don't you try one of these?

Orange & walnut

Add the finely grated zest of an orange, 3 tablespoons of marmalade and 50g of chopped walnuts.

ALLERGIES Nuts

Lemon drizzle

Press down half the mixture, spread 150g of lemon curd over the top, and then top with the rest of the oat mixture. When cooked, drizzle 50g icing sugar mixed with the juice of ½ lemon over the top of the flapjack.

Ginger & coconut

Add 2 teaspoons of ground ginger and replace 50g of oats with desiccated coconut.

5 Once cooked, remove from the oven. Leave to cool in the tin for 15 minutes, before cutting into equal squares.

Desiccated means 'dried out'.

Like this?

Not quite.

Banoffee Traybake

Banana and toffee are two delicious flavours that combine well in this light and fluffy traybake. The sticky toffee topping is made with condensed milk, butter and sugar.

> Condensed milk is used in desserts and sweets all over the world, due to its sweetness and thick consistency.

> I don't think I mix well with sticky!

Traybake ingredients

100g butter, softened
175g caster sugar
2 eggs
225g self-raising flour
1 teaspoon baking powder
2 tablespoons milk
2 ripe large bananas

For the topping

397g tin of sweetened condensed milk
50g soft dark brown sugar
50g butter
1 banana

You will need a brownie tin, 23cm x 23cm.

Makes 9 squares.

ALLERGIES

Wheat, gluten, dairy, eggs

> This is a great way to use up over-ripe bananas.

Method

1 Heat the oven to 160°C / 350°F or gas mark 4. Grease and line the brownie tin, including the sides.

2 Cream the butter and sugar together in a large mixing bowl. Beat the eggs and add to the bowl, as well as the flour, baking powder and milk. Mix together.

3 Mash the two bananas in a bowl, tip into the cake mix and stir together.

4 Scrape the cake mix into the lined tin, and place in the oven for 30–35 minutes, until golden brown and a skewer comes away cleanly. Cool, in the tin, on a wire rack.

5 To make the topping, put the condensed milk, sugar and butter into a small saucepan and heat gently until all the sugar has dissolved.

Use a fork to mash the bananas – remember to take them out of their skins first.

Now you tell me!

6 Bring the mixture to a boil (angry bubbles), stirring all the time, and then turn the heat down to a simmer (gentle little bubbles). Let the sauce cook for a few minutes until smooth and thick. Remove from the heat and let cool for 5 minutes.

7 Take the cake (still in the tin) and pour the caramel sauce over the top.

Hot caramel is very hot and very sticky, so make sure a grown-up does this bit for you!

8 Once cool, cut the banana into 9 slices, and arrange in rows on top of the cake. Use a sharp knife to cut the cake into 9 squares.

Apple Traybake

This moist cake is full of juicy apple pieces and topped with cinnamon and sugar. You can find different varieties of apple cake in many countries, including England, Poland, Sweden and the USA.

> For this recipe, prepare the apples by peeling them, then remove the cores before chopping the apples into thin slices.

> A vegetable peeler will make this easier, but you can use a knife if you're careful.

Traybake ingredients
4 large apples
½ lemon, juiced
225g butter, softened
280g caster sugar
4 eggs
2 teaspoons vanilla extract

350g self-raising flour
2 teaspoons baking powder

For the topping
50g soft light brown sugar
2 teaspoons cinnamon
(optional)

You will need a brownie tin, 23cm x 23cm.

Makes 16 squares.

ALLERGIES
Wheat, gluten, dairy, eggs

Method

1 Heat the oven to 160°C / 350°F or gas mark 4. Grease and line the brownie tin, including the sides.

2 Peel, core and thinly slice the apples and put on a plate. Squeeze the lemon juice over the apples.

> The lemon juice helps to stop the apples from going brown before you need them.

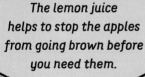

3 Cream the butter and sugar together in a large mixing bowl. Beat the eggs. Mix in the vanilla extract and add to the large bowl, along with the flour and baking powder. Mix together.

4 Tip half of the cake mix into the brownie tin and level using your wooden spoon. Arrange half of the apple slices on top of the first layer of cake mix.

5 Add the remaining cake mix and top with the rest of the apple slices. Mix the demerara sugar in a bowl with the cinnamon, if using, and sprinkle over the top apple layer.

6 Place in the oven and bake for 45–50 minutes until golden brown and a skewer comes away cleanly. Remove from the tin and cool on a wire rack. Once cool, use a sharp knife to cut into 16 squares.

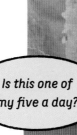

Is this one of my five a day?

Rocky Road Traybake

The earliest mention of rocky road is from Australia in 1853. Sweets sometimes spoiled on the long journey from Europe, so shopkeepers decided to melt them down and mix them with nuts and chocolate to improve their flavour. Their invention was named after the rocky roads that led to the Australian gold fields.

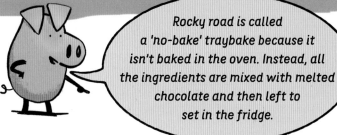

Rocky road is called a 'no-bake' traybake because it isn't baked in the oven. Instead, all the ingredients are mixed with melted chocolate and then left to set in the fridge.

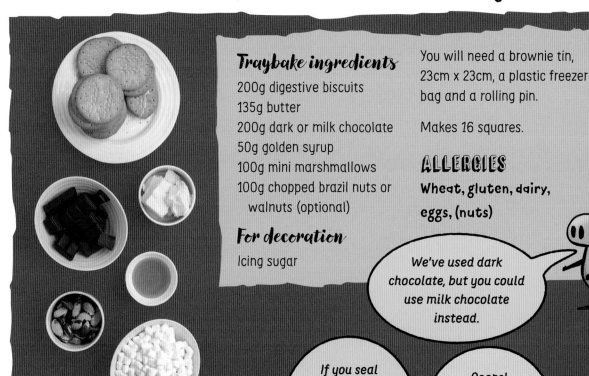

Traybake ingredients
200g digestive biscuits
135g butter
200g dark or milk chocolate
50g golden syrup
100g mini marshmallows
100g chopped brazil nuts or walnuts (optional)

For decoration
Icing sugar

You will need a brownie tin, 23cm x 23cm, a plastic freezer bag and a rolling pin.

Makes 16 squares.

ALLERGIES
Wheat, gluten, dairy, eggs, (nuts)

We've used dark chocolate, but you could use milk chocolate instead.

If you seal the bag too tightly, it might burst when you hit it with the rolling pin.

Ooops! I really should wait for Rabbit to finish talking.

Method

1 Grease and line the brownie tin, including the sides.

2 Put the biscuits into the freezer bag and tie it shut, so that air can escape, but the biscuits stay in the bag. Use the rolling pin to crush the biscuits into crumbs and some larger pieces.

3 Place the butter, chocolate and golden syrup in a large saucepan, and gently melt them all together. Stir to make sure they're all mixed in. Remove from the heat and let cool slightly. If the mixture is too hot, the marshmallows will melt!

4 Open the freezer bag and tip the biscuit crumbs into the chocolate mixture. Add the marshmallows, and nuts if you're using them. Stir together until everything is coated in chocolate.

5 Tip the mixture from the pan into the brownie tin and spread to the edges.

6 Chill in the fridge for at least 2 hours, and then cut into 16 squares. Dust with icing sugar to decorate.

The pan can be heavy, so make sure you have someone to help you.

Rocky road on a rocky road – yummy!

CORE BAKING SKILL #3 Muffins

Muffins are quick and easy to make, and can have lots of different flavours or toppings. This recipe is for classic blueberry muffins.

I like toppings!

The original muffin, or English muffin, was a flatbread baked on a griddle or hot plate and was served at teatime. It can be traced back as far as the 18th century and it was often sold by street-sellers called Muffin Men! American-style muffins are miniature cakes baked in paper cases and are flavoured with blueberries, chocolate chips or bananas.

Blueberry Muffins

Muffin ingredients

100g butter, softened
140g caster sugar
2 eggs
140g natural yoghurt
1 teaspoon vanilla extract
2 tablespoons milk
250g self-raising flour
1 teaspoon bicarbonate
   of soda
¼ teaspoon salt
125g fresh blueberries

You will need a 12-hole muffin tin and 12 muffin paper cases.

ALLERGIES

Wheat, gluten, dairy, eggs

Muffin cases are bigger than cupcake cases!

You could use chopped apple, raspberries, chocolate chips or chopped nuts instead of blueberries.

Method

1 Heat the oven to 180°C / 400°F or gas mark 6. Line the muffin tin with the paper cases.

2 Cream together the butter and sugar in a bowl until light and fluffy.

3 Add the eggs and beat together for 1 minute. Add the yoghurt, vanilla extract and milk, and whisk together.

4 Sieve the flour, bicarbonate of soda and salt into another bowl.

5 Add the flour mixture to the wet ingredients and stir with a wooden spoon until all the ingredients are combined. Add the blueberries to the bowl and gently stir again.

6 Divide the muffin mixture evenly between the 12 paper cases, coming about two-thirds of the way up the sides.

A large spoon is a good idea at this point – but be careful not to overfill the cases.

Oh!

7 Bake for 20 minutes, turning the oven down to 180°C / 350°F or gas mark 4 after 5 minutes. The muffins are baked when risen and golden, or when a skewer comes out cleanly.

Leave in the tin for 10 minutes, before moving on to a wire rack to cool completely.

Double Chocolate Muffins

You could also drizzle them with melted chocolate, or add chocolate buttercream as a topping!

These muffins use both chocolate and cocoa powder to make them extra chocolatey! The recipe also contains vegetable oil to make sure the muffins stay moist.

That would make them TRIPLE chocolate muffins! Wow!

Muffin ingredients

200g dark / milk chocolate
    or chocolate chips
250g self-raising flour
2 teaspoons baking powder
25g cocoa powder
175g caster sugar
1 egg
90ml vegetable oil
250ml milk
1 teaspoon vanilla extract

To decorate

50g dark chocolate (optional)
100g chocolate buttercream
    (optional – see page 24 for
    instructions)

You will need a 12-hole muffin tin and 12 muffin paper cases.

ALLERGIES

Wheat, gluten, dairy, eggs

Leave the chocolate in its wrapper and bash it a few times on a work surface to break it up! Or use a sharp knife.

I have my own technique!

Method

1 Heat the oven to 180°C / 400°F or gas mark 6. Line the muffin tin with paper cases.

2 If using chocolate rather than chocolate chips, break the chocolate into small pieces.

3 Put the chocolate, flour, baking powder, cocoa powder, and sugar into a bowl, and stir together.

4 In a jug, whisk the egg, oil, milk and vanilla extract.

5 Slowly add the wet ingredients to the flour mixture, until just combined.

6 Spoon the mixture into the paper cases until each case is two-thirds full.

7 Bake for 20 minutes until the muffins are risen and springy, and a skewer comes out cleanly.

8 Leave in the tin for 10 minutes, then move to a wire rack to cool completely.

9 To decorate, you can either melt some chocolate and drizzle over the top, or use some chocolate buttercream to top the muffin.

Fun Facts

Chocolate is made from the seeds of the cacao tree.

The word 'chocolate' can be traced back to the Aztec word 'xocoatl' which was a bitter drink made from cacao beans.

The first solid chocolate bar was made in 1847 by Joseph Fry, an English confectioner.

Banana and Honey Muffins

> *Bananas are a great snack on their own, but are even more delicious in these muffins.*

This recipe is a great way to use up very ripe bananas - the browner the skin the better! Sugar is replaced by honey to add a different flavour.

Muffin ingredients

25g butter
50g runny honey, plus a tablespoon for glazing
½ teaspoon vanilla extract
175g self-raising flour
½ teaspoon bicarbonate of soda
¼ teaspoon salt
2 large, very ripe bananas

You will need a 12-hole muffin tin and 12 muffin paper cases.

ALLERGIES

Wheat, gluten, dairy

Fun Facts

Bananas float in water.

Bananas are really healthy, high in fibre and potassium.

A banana completed the Barcelona Marathon in under 3 hours.

> *Okay, it was a man inside a banana costume!*

Method

1 Heat the oven to 170°C / 375°F or gas mark 5. Line the muffin tin with paper cases.

2 Put the butter and honey into a small pan and heat gently on the hob, until the butter has melted. Take off the heat and let cool slightly before adding the vanilla extract.

3 Combine the flour, bicarbonate of soda and salt in a bowl. Mash the bananas in another bowl. Add the honey mixture to the bananas and stir together.

4 Add the banana mixture to the flour and stir again until the flour is just mixed in.

Don't worry if it looks lumpy and bumpy – it's supposed to.

I'm lumpy and bumpy too – we match!

5 Spoon the mixture into the paper cases until each case is two-thirds full.

6 Bake for 20–25 minutes until the muffins have risen and are springy, and a skewer comes out cleanly. Leave to stand in the tin for 10 minutes before taking out to cool further on a wire rack. To finish, drizzle runny honey over the muffins.

The word 'biscuit' comes from Latin and Old French and means 'twice-baked'. In the past, biscuits were baked twice to become hard so that they could be easily carried and would last a long time on journeys.

They didn't taste very nice though, so cooks started experimenting with spices and sugar to make their biscuits more tasty and appealing.

Gingerbread Biscuits

In the Middle Ages, spices and sugar were very expensive and only wealthy people could afford to enjoy spicy cakes. Gingerbread biscuits started life as a way to use up leftover cake mix, making biscuits flavoured with spices more affordable for the less wealthy.

These days, gingerbread biscuits can be any shape, and are decorated with icing patterns and sprinkles. They are particularly popular during holidays.

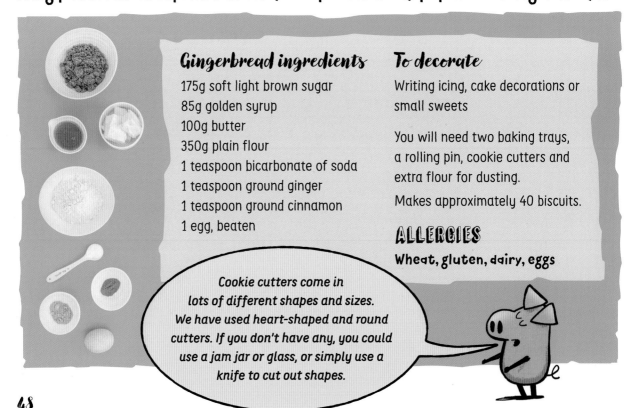

Gingerbread ingredients

175g soft light brown sugar
85g golden syrup
100g butter
350g plain flour
1 teaspoon bicarbonate of soda
1 teaspoon ground ginger
1 teaspoon ground cinnamon
1 egg, beaten

To decorate

Writing icing, cake decorations or small sweets

You will need two baking trays, a rolling pin, cookie cutters and extra flour for dusting.

Makes approximately 40 biscuits.

ALLERGIES

Wheat, gluten, dairy, eggs

Cookie cutters come in lots of different shapes and sizes. We have used heart-shaped and round cutters. If you don't have any, you could use a jam jar or glass, or simply use a knife to cut out shapes.

Method

1 Put the sugar, golden syrup and butter into a pan, and heat gently on the hob until everything has dissolved. Let the mixture bubble for 1–2 minutes and then take off the heat and leave to cool for about 10 minutes.

Ask a grown-up to help you with this, as the mixture will be very hot!

2 Put the flour, bicarbonate of soda and spices into a large bowl, and make a hole in the middle of the ingredients.

3 Carefully tip the warm syrup mixture into the hole and then add the egg.

4 Stir everything together. It will begin to form a ball. Using your hands, knead the dough gently until it is smooth and all the same colour.

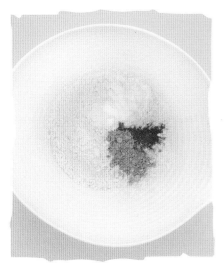

Kneading is a really useful skill to practise. Use your fingers to squeeze the dough together. Keep squishing it into a ball, making sure you catch all the crumbs.

5 Wrap the ball of dough in cling film and put in the fridge for at least 30 minutes.

6 Take the dough out of the fridge to come up to room temperature, and heat the oven to 170°C / 375°F or gas mark 5. Line two baking trays with greaseproof paper.

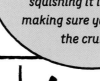

7 Dust your work surface and rolling pin with flour. Roll out the dough so it is 5mm thick. If the dough seems sticky, add a little more flour to the surface.

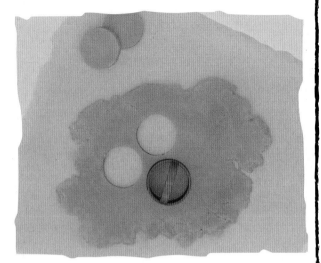

8 Use your cutters to press out all the biscuits you can fit into the dough. Then carefully gather up the 'in-between' bits, leaving the biscuits on the work surface. Carefully lift the biscuits on to the baking trays, using a palette knife or fish slice. Make sure that there is some space around them.

Gather up the scraps into a ball, and keep re-rolling and cutting until you've used all the dough.

9 Place the baking trays in the oven and cook for 10–12 minutes. It's a good idea to swap the trays over halfway through, so that the biscuits cook evenly.

To check your biscuits are cooked, simply touch them with your finger to see if they are firm! Don't use a skewer here!

10 When the biscuits are cooked, leave them to cool on the trays for 5 minutes and then carefully transfer them to a wire rack to cool completely before decorating.

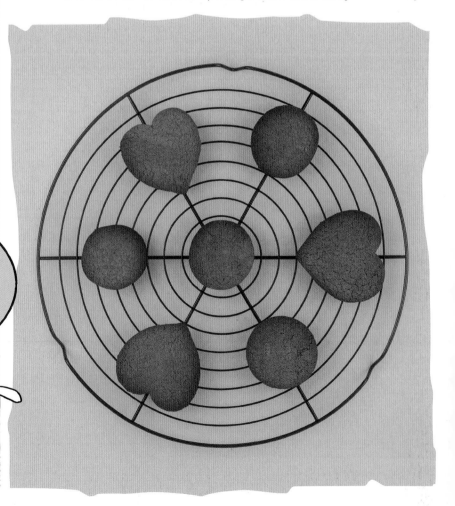

Ask a grown-up to help you!

11 Use the writing icing and sweets and sprinkles to make your biscuits look pretty, and leave to set for 1–2 hours.

For tips on icing check out page 110.

I could do with some tips!

Oops!

Fun Facts

Ginger comes from South-east Asia.

Ginger is a rhizome, not a root. A rhizome is an underground stem.

Ginger is really good for you, especially for soothing your tummy.

Perfect for you, Sheep, when you've eaten too much!

Who, me? I never overeat!

Shortbread

Shortbread is a traditional Scottish biscuit made of only three ingredients – flour, butter and sugar. It has a crumbly texture and is usually baked in small rounds, rectangular 'fingers' or triangular petticoat tails, which are made by baking a large circle and then cutting it into pieces like a pizza.

> You can use shortbread to make any shape you want – stars are pretty. Or decorate with chocolate or icing.

Shortbread ingredients

100g butter, chilled
150g plain flour
50g caster sugar, plus 1 tablespoon for sprinkling

You will need a baking tray, cutters and a rolling pin, plus extra flour for dusting.

Makes approximately 15 shortbread rounds.

ALLERGIES

Wheat, gluten, dairy

Method

1 Heat the oven to 150°C / 335°F or gas mark 3. Line the tray with baking parchment.

2 Cut the butter into small pieces and put in a mixing bowl with the flour.

3 Use the rubbing in method (see page 61), until the mixture looks like breadcrumbs.

4 Stir in the sugar, then use your hands to bring the mixture together in a ball.

> The butter softens with the heat of your hands, so it sticks together well.

> I think Rabbit might be better at this than me!

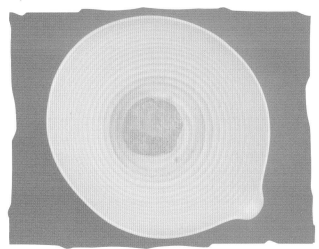

5 Sprinkle some flour on your work surface, and roll out the dough until it is 5mm thick.

6 Use your chosen cutter shape to press into the dough. Move the biscuits to the baking tray, leaving a space between them and sprinkle with the leftover sugar.

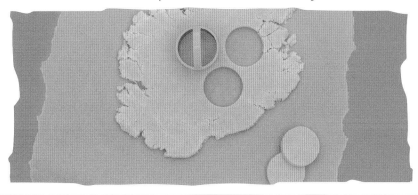

7 Bake in the oven for 15–20 minutes until golden brown. Once cooked, leave to cool on the baking tray for 10 minutes, so they firm up before you move them.

Savoury Cheese Biscuits

I love cheese! Especially Edam because it's made backwards.

Biscuits were originally savoury in flavour. These cheese biscuits are great for picnics or a morning snack, if you don't have a sweet tooth!

Biscuit ingredients

100g wholemeal flour
50g plain flour
25g rolled oats
100g butter, chilled
100g cheddar cheese
1 egg

You will need a baking tray and a rolling pin, plus extra flour for dusting.

Makes 12–14 biscuits.

ALLERGIES
Wheat, gluten, dairy, eggs

Method

1 Heat the oven to 160°C / 350°F or gas mark 4. Line a baking tray with baking parchment.

2 Cut the butter into small pieces and put it in a mixing bowl with both flours and the oatmeal. Rub the butter in (see page 61), until the mixture looks like breadcrumbs.

3 Finely grate the cheese, and then add it to the mixture.

4 Add the egg and stir using a fork. Once the mixture starts to come together, use your hands to bring the mixture together in a ball.

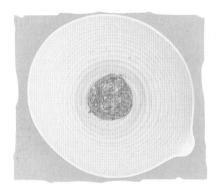

5 Sprinkle some flour on your work surface and roll out the dough until it is 5mm thick. Try to roll it into a large rectangle.

6 Cut into rectangles so each biscuit is approximately 7cm x 2cm in size. Place the rectangles on the baking tray.

7 Bake in the oven for 20–25 minutes until golden brown. Once cooked, leave the biscuits to cool on the baking tray for 10 minutes, so they firm up before you move them on to a cooling rack.

You can make variations by adding herbs or spices to change the flavours. Try one of these! Make sure you only use the leaves of the rosemary though, and not the stalk!

Black olive and rosemary

Add the following to the mixture, before adding the egg.
- 2 sprigs of fresh rosemary, finely chopped
- 20g black olives, finely chopped

Parmesan and hazelnut

Substitute the cheddar for 75g parmesan.
Add 20g hazelnuts, finely chopped before you add the egg.

Walnut and raisin

Add the following to the mixture, before adding the egg.
- 20g raisins, finely chopped
- 20g walnuts, finely chopped

Chocolate Chip Cookies

A cookie is a different type of biscuit. It is softer and has a chewy texture. The name itself is thought to come from the Dutch for 'little cake'.

Cookies are made by the 'drop' method. You simply drop a spoonful of mixture onto the baking tray, and it spreads to form a round shape.

Cookie ingredients

100g butter, softened
75g caster sugar
75g soft light brown sugar
1 egg
1 teaspoon vanilla extract
175g plain flour
½ teaspoon bicarbonate of soda

150g chocolate chips (dark, milk or white)

You will need two baking trays.

Makes 16–20 cookies.

ALLERGIES

Wheat, gluten, dairy, eggs

If you don't have any chocolate chips, you can chop up a bar into pieces.

Method

1 Heat the oven to 160°C / 350°F or gas mark 4. Grease and line two baking trays.

2 Cream the butter and both sugars together in a bowl until smooth.

3 Add the egg and the vanilla extract, and beat until creamy.

4 Sift the plain flour and bicarbonate of soda into the same bowl, and stir with a wooden spoon until all mixed together. Add the chocolate chips and stir again.

Only one bowl for this recipe! Much less washing up!

5 Use two teaspoons to dollop ping-pong ball-sized amounts of mixture on to the baking trays, making sure to leave space in between the cookies.

If you don't leave enough space, they will join together while baking, forming a ginormous cookie!

6 Bake in the oven for 10–12 minutes until golden. They should still be slightly squidgy in the middle.

7 Leave them on the tray for 5 minutes to set, before moving on to a cooling rack.

And that's a problem because...?

Peanut Butter Cookies

These cookies are nutty and sweet at the same time, and are delicious as a snack. Peanut butter can be smooth or it can be crunchy. This recipe uses the crunchy variety.

Some people are allergic to nuts. Don't share these cookies with friends without checking.

Cookie ingredients

75g butter, softened
50g crunchy peanut butter
75g caster sugar
75g soft light brown sugar
1 egg
1 teaspoon vanilla extract
175g plain flour
½ teaspoon bicarbonate of soda
50g unsalted peanuts, chopped

You will need two baking trays.

Makes 12 cookies.

ALLERGIES

Wheat, gluten, dairy, eggs, nuts

Use a sharp knife and chopping board to chop your peanuts.

Make sure you have a tea towel under your board and a grown-up nearby.

Fun Facts

It takes approximately 540 peanuts to make one jar of peanut butter.

US president Thomas Jefferson was a peanut farmer.

Peanut butter and jam, or jelly, is a popular sandwich filling in the USA.

Method

1 Heat the oven to 150°C / 325°F or gas mark 3. Grease and line two baking trays.

2 Cream the butter, peanut butter and both sugars together in a bowl until smooth.

3 Add the egg and the vanilla extract, and beat until creamy.

I love cookies!

4 Sieve the flour and bicarbonate of soda into the bowl, and then add the chopped peanuts. Stir with a wooden spoon until all mixed together.

5 Use two teaspoons to dollop ping-pong-ball-sized amounts of mixture on to the baking trays, making sure to leave space in between them.

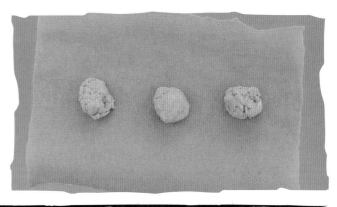

6 Bake in the oven for 10–12 minutes until golden. They should be firm around the edges, but still be slightly squidgy in the middle.

I'm nuts about baking!

7 Leave them on the tray for 5 minutes to set before moving to a wire rack to cool.

CORE RECIPE
#5 Shortcrust Pastry

There are lots of different types of pastry including shortcrust, puff and filo. Puff pastry and filo pastry are often easier to buy ready-made and do save time when baking. However, once you know how to make a basic shortcrust pastry, then you'll be amazed at what you can make. Tarts and pies of all descriptions – savoury and sweet – are made with a simple mixture of flour, fat and water, and a little bit of elbow grease...

I don't think I have the right sort of elbows to make pastry to tell you the hoof!

Jam Tarts

Pastry ingredients
150g plain flour
75g cold butter
Cold water
Plus extra flour for dusting

For the filling
12 teaspoons raspberry or apricot jam

You will need a rolling pin, a 12-hole shallow bun tin and a 6cm pastry cutter.

ALLERGIES
Wheat, gluten, dairy

Can't decide which jam is your favourite? Why not have two flavours?

Method
To make the pastry

1 Sift the flour into a large mixing bowl. Cut the butter into small chunks, about the size of grapes, and then use the rubbing in method (see page 61) to create a breadcrumb-like mixture.

Rubbing in method

1. Using the very tips of your fingers (otherwise the butter can start to melt), pinch some flour and butter together, and then rub the mixture between your fingers three times.

2. Drop it back into the bowl and pinch some more.

3. Keep pinching and rubbing until all the flour and butter have combined into a crumb-like mixture.

If your hands are very warm, run them under the cold tap for 10 seconds to cool them down first!

2 Add 2 tablespoons of cold water to the bowl. Using a blunt knife, bring the mixture together. If the mixture seems too dry, you can always add more water. Once the breadcrumb mix has started to come together, use your hands to bring it into a ball.

3 Pastry needs to rest and cool down for 20 minutes once it has been made, so cover it in cling film and pop it in the fridge.

I need to cool down too!

Method
To make the jam tarts

1 Heat the oven to 160°C / 350°F or gas mark 4. Lightly grease a shallow bun tin with butter.

2 Sprinkle your work surface with some flour. Unwrap the pastry from the cling film and put it in the middle of the work surface.

Make sure it is clean and dry before you sprinkle the flour!

3 Using your hands, press down on the pastry ball to flatten it. Make sure it moves easily on the surface. Next, take your rolling pin, and roll out the pastry until it is about 3mm thick.

Rolling out pastry

1. Take a rolling pin and gently press down on the pastry, while rolling the pin over the pastry once or twice.

2. Pick up the pastry and turn it 90°.

3. Roll again two or three times, then spin the pastry again. By moving the pastry around, you are making sure that it doesn't stick to the surface and that it is being rolled out evenly.

If you want to make a circle, start with a ball. If you want to make a rectangle, start with a block. Add a little more flour if the pastry starts to stick.

4 Use your cutter to cut out pastry circles and put one into each of the holes in the bun tin. Gather up the leftover pastry into a ball and flatten. Roll the pastry out again and keep cutting circles until you can't fit the cutter on any more.

Pastry cutters usually have a smooth edge, or a pretty scalloped edge if you flip them over. You can use whichever side you like!

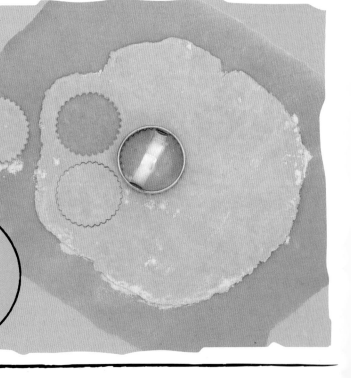

5 Gather up the final scraps of leftover pastry and form into a small ball. Use the ball to push the tart cases down, so you don't poke your finger through the pastry when pressing them into the tin.

6 Prick the base of the tarts with a fork a few times to stop the pastry puffing up. Spoon in 1 teaspoon of jam per tart. Put in the oven for 15 minutes or until golden brown.

7 When the tarts are ready, the pastry will be crisp and light brown on the bottom. Leave to cool before eating.

Apple Pie

There are lots of different types of apples you can use, including Braeburn, Bramley, Gala or Granny Smith!

Apple pies are old! The first written recipe for apple pie was recorded by Chaucer (a 14th-century English author), so we have been enjoying apple pies for a very long time. This recipe is a simple closed pie with a lovely apple filling. Cinnamon is optional!

I don't approve of taking fruit from old ladies. Leave that granny alone!

Pastry ingredients

320g plain flour
160g cold butter
Cold water

For the filling

1kg apples
2 tablespoons soft light brown sugar
1 tablespoon plain flour
1 teaspoon cinnamon

For the topping

2 tablespoons milk
1 tablespoon soft light brown sugar

You will need a rolling pin and a pie dish, 20cm-diameter.

ALLERGIES

Wheat, gluten, dairy

Method

1 Sift the flour into a large bowl. Cut the butter into small chunks and then use the rubbing in method (see page 61) to create a crumb-like mixture.

2 Add 5 or 6 tablespoons of cold water and mix until it comes together. Split the mixture into two balls – a small one which is a third of the mixture, and a larger one which is two-thirds. Wrap both balls individually in cling film and put in the fridge to rest for 30 minutes.

3 Heat the oven to 180°C / 400°F or gas mark 6. Lightly grease the pie dish with some butter.

4 Prepare the apples by peeling them with a vegetable peeler. Cut the apples in quarters, and remove the core with a sharp knife. Chop the apples into 1cm-thick slices. Place in a bowl and mix with the sugar, flour and cinnamon.

You might have an apple corer which takes the whole core out in one go. Be careful, though!

5 Take the pastry out of the fridge. Roll the larger ball into a circle 5cm bigger in diameter than the pie dish. Carefully roll the pastry onto the rolling pin, and move it over the pie dish. Unroll the pastry and gently push it into the bottom of the dish.

This is called 'crimping' the edges and seals the pastry case shut.

6 Tip the apple mixture into the pie case. Using a pastry brush, paint milk around the edge of the pastry.

7 Roll out the small ball of pastry a little larger than the top of the pie. Lift the pastry circle on top of the dish, and press down to seal the pie. Use a sharp knife or scissors to trim off the edges. Use a fork to press a shape into the edge.

I thought that was something you did to your hair!

8 Use a knife to make three or four small slits in the top of the pastry so steam can escape. Brush all over with milk and sprinkle with the brown sugar.

9 Bake in the oven for 45–55 minutes, or until golden brown all over. Serve with cream, ice cream or custard.

Or, even better, all three!

Cheese and Onion Quiche

That's not what baking blind means, Sheep!

A quiche is a lovely savoury tart with an egg custard filling and can be eaten warm or cold. To make sure that the filling doesn't soak through, the pastry case is baked blind for 10 minutes.

Now he tells me...

Pastry ingredients
320g plain flour
160g cold butter
Cold water

For the filling
5 small onions
25g butter
2 eggs
284ml double cream
140g cheddar cheese, grated
Salt and pepper

You will need a rolling pin and a 23cm tart tin, baking parchment, ceramic baking beans or dried peas or rice.

ALLERGIES
Wheat, gluten, dairy, eggs

Sometimes chopping onions can make your eyes water. Use a sharp knife, and make sure the onions are cold. Just don't rub your eyes!

Method

1 Sift the flour into a large mixing bowl. Cut the butter into small chunks and use the rubbing-in method (see page 61) to create a crumb-like mixture.

2 Add 5 or 6 tablespoons of cold water and mix until it comes together. Add more water if you need to. Wrap in cling film and put in the fridge to rest for 20 minutes.

3 Prepare the onions by removing the brown outer skin. Chop them in half and slice thinly.

4 In a frying pan, melt the butter and add the onions. Cook them over a medium heat for 20 minutes, until golden brown and sticky, stirring occasionally.

5 Lightly grease the tart tin. Take the pastry out of the fridge. Roll out into a circle 5cm bigger in diameter than the tart tin. Carefully lift the pastry over the tin and push it into the bottom edges of the dish. Put back in the fridge for 20 minutes. Heat the oven to 180°C / 400°F or gas mark 6.

6 Take the pastry case out of the fridge. Prick the bottom of the case with a fork. Lay the baking parchment on top and tip in the baking beans to form a single layer.

The baking beans keep the pastry flat while it cooks.

7 Bake the pastry for 20 minutes. Then, remove the paper and beans and continue for another 10 minutes until the pastry is golden brown. This is baking blind.

Carefully!

8 Make the quiche filling by beating the eggs in a bowl. Add the double cream, onions and half the grated cheese. Season with a pinch of salt and pepper.

9 Tip the filling into the pastry case and sprinkle over the rest of the cheese. Cook in the oven for 20 minutes until set and golden. Leave to cool in the case.

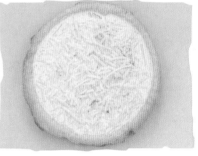

10 Once cool, take a sharp knife and trim the edges of the pastry around the tart case to make it neat. Take the quiche out of the tin, cut into slices and serve.

Salt is often added to make food taste more flavourful. Careful, though, too much can taste horrible!

67

Pecan Pie

Pecan pie comes from the USA – particularly the south where pecan nuts grow on hickory trees. Created in the late 19th century, the pie is often eaten during Thanksgiving and Christmas celebrations.

Pastry ingredients
280g plain flour
140g cold butter
Cold water

For the filling
75g butter, softened
100g caster sugar
175g golden syrup
175g maple syrup
3 eggs
½ teaspoon vanilla
  extract

300g pecan halves
Double cream, to serve

You will need a rolling pin and a 23cm tart tin, baking parchment, ceramic baking beans or dried peas or rice.

ALLERGIES
Wheat, gluten, dairy, eggs, nuts

Fun Facts

Pecan nuts grow in the Mississippi River region of the USA and in Mexico.

A pecan tree can live for more than 200 years.

There are over 1,000 varieties of pecan nuts.

That's a lot of nuts!

Method

1 Rub the butter into the flour in a large mixing bowl and add 5 or 6 tablespoons of cold water. Mix until it comes together in a ball. Wrap in cling film and put in the fridge for 20 minutes.

2 Lightly grease the tart tin. Roll out into a circle 5cm bigger in diameter than the tin. Line the tin with the pastry, and put back in the fridge for another 20 minutes.

3 Heat the oven to 170°C / 375°F or gas mark 5. Lightly prick the pastry with a fork. Lay the baking parchment and beans on top. Blind-bake the tart for 20 minutes. Remove the paper and beans. Bake for 10 minutes until the pastry is golden brown.

4 Increase the oven temperature to 180°C / 400°F or gas mark 6. Make the pie filling by beating the butter and sugar in a bowl until light and fluffy. Gradually add both syrups and use a whisk to mix thoroughly.

Be careful!

Maple syrup comes from the maple tree, and it takes 40 litres of tree sap to make 1 litre of syrup.

5 Beat the eggs in a bowl. Slowly add the eggs to the syrup mixture. Add a pinch of salt and the vanilla extract. Stir in the pecan halves and pour into the tart case.

Don't overfill the tart case! Be careful when you're putting it in the oven, as the mixture is quite runny!

6 Bake for 10 minutes, and then turn the oven down to 150°C / 325°F or gas mark 3. Bake for 30–35 minutes until set and golden. Leave to cool in the case.

7 Trim the pastry edges. Take the tart out of the tin, cut into slices and serve with whipped cream.

Pecan pie is my favourite!

CORE BAKING SKILL
#6 Cheesecake

I love cheese!

Cheesecakes can be found all over the world. Almost every country has a slightly different version of this biscuit-based, sweet, cream cheese dessert.

New York Vanilla Cheesecake

Biscuit base ingredients

175g digestive biscuits
75g butter

For the filling

600g full-fat cream cheese, room temperature
200g caster sugar
25g plain flour
2 large eggs
2 teaspoons vanilla extract
100ml sour cream

For the topping

50ml sour cream

You will need a 23cm spring-form cake tin.

ALLERGIES

Wheat, gluten, dairy, eggs, nuts

A spring-form tin is one that is clipped into place while cooking and can be unclipped afterwards. It makes it much easier to get the cheesecake out in one piece.

Make sure the tin is clipped correctly, or the mixture will leak out!

Method

1 Heat the oven to 160°C / 350°F or gas mark 4. Grease and line the spring-form cake tin, including the sides.

2 To make the crumb base, you need to crush the digestive biscuits. The best way to do this is to place them in a plastic bag and bash them with a rolling pin. Hold the end of the bag so the crumbs don't make a mess.

These should be fine crumbs without lumps, otherwise it can be hard to cut the cheesecake to serve.

Mind your fingers!

3 Melt the butter in a pan. Take the pan off the heat and then add the crumbs. Mix with a wooden spoon until all the crumbs are coated in butter.

4 Tip the crumb mixture into the cake tin and carefully push to the edge. Flatten the crumbs with the back of the spoon, so you have a smooth, even layer.

5 Put the cake tin into the oven for 10 mins to bake firm. Then, let the crumb base cool completely in the tin, while you make the filling.

6 Put the cream cheese in a large bowl and beat to loosen. Add the sugar gradually before adding the flour. Mix again.

7 Beat the eggs in a smaller bowl, add the vanilla extract, and stir.

8 Using a wooden spoon, add a little of the egg mixture to the cream cheese bowl and mix together until combined. Repeat until all the egg mixture is used up.

9 Using a whisk, add the sour cream and whisk again until the mixture looks light and airy.

If there are any lumps, use a spoon to push them against the side of the bowl to smooth them out.

10 Pour the cheese mixture into the cake tin, and smooth out the top. Put into the oven.

11 After 10 minutes, turn the oven down to 110°C / 260°F or gas mark ½. Bake the cheesecake for a further 30 minutes. There should be a slight wobble on the surface.

Ask a grown-up to check for you!

12 Turn off the oven. Leave the cheesecake in for another 30 minutes. This helps to prevent cracks forming on the surface.

13 Take it out of the oven and leave it to cool on a wire rack, and then put it in the fridge for at least 2 hours.

14 To remove it from the tin, run a round-bladed knife around its edge. Carefully release the clip and the tin should come away from the sides of the set cheesecake. Slide the dessert off the tin base and remove the baking parchment from the sides and base.

15 Finally, just before serving, spoon over the 50ml of sour cream and spread to the edges of the cheesecake.

This will be delicious with some fresh fruit such as strawberries or blueberries!

I'm afraid we're fresh out of strawberries! They... erm... went bad...

Fun Facts

Baked American cheesecakes were invented during the 1870s.

The biggest ever cheesecake weighed 4,240kg.

Cheesecakes were used as wedding cakes in ancient Greece.

Lemon Cheesecake

This is a deliciously tangy cheesecake that uses lemon curd and sour cream to make a lovely topping.

Lemon curd is a lemon spread made from lemon juice, butter, sugar and eggs. We have used a ready-made one for this recipe.

Biscuit base ingredients
175g digestive biscuit crumbs
85g butter

For the filling
600g full-fat cream cheese, room temperature
200g caster sugar
25g plain flour
2 large eggs
100ml sour cream

2 lemons (both zested, 1 juiced), (see page 23 for instructions)

For the topping
100ml sour cream
3 tablespoons lemon curd

You will need a 20cm spring-form cake tin.

ALLERGIES
Wheat, gluten, dairy, eggs

Method

1 Heat the oven to 160°C / 350°F or gas mark 4. Grease and line the spring-form cake tin, including the sides.

2 Melt the butter in a pan and then add the digestive crumbs and mix. Tip the crumb mixture into the cake tin and carefully push to the edge. Flatten the crumbs with the back of the spoon, so you have a flat layer.

3 Put the cake tin into the oven for 10 minutes to bake firm. Let it cool completely in the tin, while you make the filling.

4 Put the cream cheese in a large bowl and beat to loosen. Add the sugar gradually before adding the flour. Beat the eggs in a smaller bowl.

5 Gradually add the egg mixture to the cream cheese and mix together. Using a whisk, add the sour cream, lemon zest and juice and whisk again until the mixture looks light and airy.

6 Pour the cheese mixture into the tin. Put into the oven. After 10 minutes, turn the oven down to 110°C / 260°F or gas mark ½. Bake the cheesecake for a further 30 minutes until there is a slight wobble on the surface.

Ask a grown-up to check for you!

7 Turn off the oven. Leave the cheesecake in for another 30 minutes. Take it out of the oven and leave it to cool on a wire rack. Then put it in the fridge for at least 2 hours.

Spread the word, I love curd!

8 Remove from the tin (see page 72 for instructions) and decorate by spooning over the remaining sour cream and then swirling the lemon curd on top.

No-bake Raspberry Cheesecake

> No baking?
> This sounds more
> promising!

A much easier cheesecake to make is the 'no-bake' kind!
The recipe doesn't use eggs, but uses whipped cream instead.
To make the cheesecake fruity and tasty, raspberry purée is
rippled through the delicious cream cheese topping.

Biscuit base ingredients

175g digestive biscuit crumbs
75g butter

For the raspberry purée

300g raspberries (fresh or frozen)
25g caster sugar
50ml water

For the filling

600g full-fat cream cheese, room temperature
200g caster sugar
225ml double or whipping cream, room temperature

You will need a 23cm spring-form cake tin.

ALLERGIES

Wheat, gluten, dairy

Raspberry Purée

1. Put the raspberries, sugar and water in a medium pan. Cook over a low heat until the raspberries have broken down and the sugar has dissolved. Simmer for 20 minutes to thicken slightly. Remove from the heat to cool.

2. Place a sieve over a bowl. Carefully tip the purée into the sieve. Using a metal spoon, push the purée through the sieve to remove the seeds. Keep the purée in a clean jam jar in the fridge until needed. It will last for 3 days.

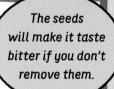

> The seeds will make it taste bitter if you don't remove them.

> You may need a grown-up for this bit.

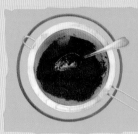

Method

1 First, make the raspberry purée.

2 Line the base and sides of the spring-form cake tin.

3 Melt the butter in a pan and then add the digestive crumbs and mix. Tip the crumb mixture into the cake tin and flatten until smooth and even. Put the tin in the fridge for at least 30 minutes to set firm.

4 To make the filling, put the cream cheese in a large bowl and beat to loosen. Add the sugar and mix. In another bowl, whip the cream until nice and stiff and add to the cream cheese mixture.

Don't whip the cream for too long, or it will turn into butter!

5 Swirl the raspberry purée through the cream cheese.

6 Pour the cheesecake mixture into the cake tin and smooth out the top. Put into the fridge for at least 3 hours. When ready to serve, unclip from the cake tin and remove the baking parchment.

We're also out of raspberries because... never mind!

Key Lime Pie

Key lime pie isn't a cheesecake!

Key lime pie is a traditional American dessert. It is named after a variety of lime grown in the Florida Keys. The limes are different to the ones we normally see in the shops, as they have thinner skin and yellow juice. This recipe uses the more familiar limes, as they are much easier to find.

No it's not, but it does have the same biscuit base!

Biscuit base ingredients
250g digestive biscuit crumbs
125g butter

For the filling
397g tin of condensed milk
3 egg yolks (see page 110 for hints on how to separate egg yolks)
4 limes

For decoration
300ml double or whipping cream
1 tablespoon icing sugar

You will need a 23cm tart tin.

ALLERGIES
Wheat, gluten, dairy, eggs

Method

1 Heat the oven to 150°C / 325°F or gas mark 3.

2 Melt the butter in a pan and then add the digestive crumbs and mix. Tip the crumb mixture into the cake tin and carefully push it up the sides of the tin. Flatten the crumbs with the back of the spoon so you have a smooth layer.

We use the biscuit crumb mixture as pastry for this recipe. Make sure it is pressed firmly around the sides.

3 Put the tart tin into the oven for 10 minutes to bake firm. Let it cool completely in the tin while you make the filling.

4 Put the 3 egg yolks in a large bowl and beat with a whisk. Add the condensed milk and whisk for 3 minutes.

5 Finely zest the 4 limes and then squeeze them for their juice.

Roll the limes on a hard surface for 30 seconds. Cut the lime in half, and carefully use a fork to twist in the lime to release the juice. Or use a juicer.

All this whisking is good for the muscles!

6 Add the juice and zest to the egg mixture and whisk for another 3 minutes. Keep back 2 teaspoons of lime zest for decoration.

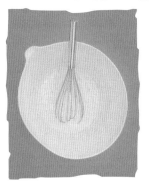

7 Pour the mixture into the cake tin and bake in the oven for 15 minutes until the filling is set. Chill for at least 3 hours before serving.

8 To decorate, whip the cream and icing sugar together in a bowl, and spoon on to the pie. Sprinkle over the remaining lime zest and serve.

Pig thinks he's an expert baker, but he left the keys out of that recipe completely!

CORE BAKING SKILL
#7 Bread

There are so many different types of bread – French baguette, Indian naan, German pumpernickel, New York bagel, Mexican tortilla, Italian panettone...

Homemade bread is easy to make. It's a simple combination of flour and water, with a little yeast thrown in, if you like. Bread can take a little more time than other recipes, as you often need to let the dough rise, or prove, before you bake it in the oven. This core recipe is for a bread loaf – white or wholemeal – using yeast to help the bread rise.

I love bread! Dough you'll have to just crust me on that...

White and Wholemeal Loaf

Dough ingredients
21g dried yeast (3 x 7g sachets)
30g caster sugar
625ml tepid water
1kg strong white flour
20g salt

You will need 2 loaf tins, some extra flour for dusting, cling film and some vegetable oil.

ALLERGIES
Wheat, gluten

Method

1 In a measuring jug, add the tepid water and mix in the yeast and the sugar, until the sugar has dissolved and the yeast starts to bubble.

Tepid is warm, but not hot! It should feel the same temperature as your hand.

1 Put the flour and salt in a large mixing bowl, and give it a stir to mix the salt into the flour. Make a well in the centre of the flour and pour in the yeast mixture.

3 Using a fork, start to bring the flour into the middle of the bowl by circling round the flour at the edges. Continue until nearly all of the flour has been worked into a moist dough.

Make sure your work surface is clean before you start the next step!

4 Then the messy bit! Tip all of the dough and any loose flour on to your work surface.

5 Using both hands, start to knead the dough. If the dough is too sticky, dust a little more flour on top and carry on.

Kneading is great. You push and pull and stretch the dough, making sure to gather all the stray bits of flour and dough on the work surface. Kneading helps to make the bread rise.

This was always going to be a problem, wasn't it?

Kneading Technique

1. Once the dough is in a rough ball shape, use your knuckles or the heels of your hands to push the dough away from you.

2. Fold the dough in half, rotate it and then push away again.

3. Repeat until the dough feels smooth and elastic. This could take up to 10 minutes.

6 Put the dough back in the mixing bowl and cover with cling film rubbed with a little oil. This stops the dough sticking to the covering. Leave to prove in a warm, draught-free place for at least 45 minutes.

In the winter, the best place is in front of a radiator.

7 While you wait, lightly grease the two loaf tins with vegetable oil. Once the dough has doubled in size, scrape the dough out of the bowl on to the work surface and knead again for 1 minute. This stage is called 'knocking back' as you are knocking the air out of the dough.

8 Using a knife, cut the dough in half. Shape each half into a long oval shape and place in the loaf tins. Cover with oiled cling film, and leave to prove for a second time for 30 minutes or until the loaves have doubled in size. While you wait, heat the oven to 200°C / 425°F or gas mark 7.

Put your loaves into the oven to bake for 30 minutes until golden.

The best way to tell if your loaf is cooked is to tap the base of the loaf. If it is ready, it will sound hollow. Don't use that skewer!

Not that kind of base, Sheep!

Wholemeal loaf

To make a wholemeal loaf, simply replace the strong white flour with strong wholemeal flour. You might need a little more water, as wholemeal flour absorbs more liquid. You could also use half white and half wholemeal flour, for a slightly lighter brown loaf.

Pizza Dough

Once you know how to make bread, there are lots of cool things you can make – including pizza dough! Simply top with tomato sauce and cheese, and you have a Pizza Margherita! Although there have been flatbreads since Roman times, pizza as we know it comes from 18th-century Naples, Italy.

You can make mini pizzas, or large rectangular pizzas that you can cut up and share with all your friends.

I'm not sure this is getting any easier!

Dough ingredients
10g dried yeast
15g caster sugar
300ml tepid water
500g strong white flour
1 teaspoon salt

You will need 3 baking trays, a rolling pin, some extra flour for dusting, and olive oil.

ALLERGIES
Wheat, gluten

Method

1 In a measuring jug, add the tepid water and mix in the yeast and the sugar, until the sugar has dissolved and the yeast starts to bubble.

2 Put the flour and salt in a large mixing bowl. Make a well in the centre of the flour and pour in the yeast mixture. Stir the flour into the liquid, until it has been worked into a moist dough.

3 Tip the dough on to a work surface and knead for 10 minutes. (See page 81 for method.) Once smooth and elastic, put back in the bowl and cover with oiled cling film to prove, until doubled in size.

4 While you wait, heat the oven to 200°C / 425°F or gas mark 7. Prepare your baking trays by lightly oiling them, and then dust with flour.

Tomato Sauce

Sauce ingredients

1 clove of garlic
1 tablespoon olive oil
2 teaspoons dried oregano
1 tablespoon tomato purée

2 x 400g tins of chopped tomatoes
Salt and pepper for seasoning

You will need a pan and garlic crusher or sharp knife.

> You can also make your tomato sauce!

Fun Facts

Tomatoes were first brought to Europe from South America in the 16th century.

They were originally yellow.

Tomatoes increase in weight as they ripen.

5 Put the pan on the hob on a low heat, and add the oil. Crush or chop the garlic and add to the pan. Stir as the garlic softens.

6 Add the dried oregano and tomato purée, and stir.

7 Finally add the tins of tomatoes and season. Cook for 30 minutes over a slow heat, stirring occasionally, until the sauce gets nice and thick. Leave to cool.

> If you don't have a garlic crusher, simply take the skin off the garlic clove and chop into tiny pieces.

8 Once the dough has doubled in size, knock it back (see page 82 for method) and divide into three balls.

9 Dust your work surface with more flour. Take one of the balls and roll it out, turning a quarter circle with every roll until the pizza is about 5mm thick and 30cm in diameter.

The dough is really stretchy and will want to spring back, so you need to roll quite hard.

10 Place the rolled out pizza on a baking tray and leave for 5–10 minutes to puff up slightly. Repeat with the other two balls of dough. Then add your toppings.

11 Spoon over the tomato sauce.

11 Choose any pizza topping that you like to make your pizza, making sure you sprinkle it with mozzerella cheese first. Cook in the oven for 12–15 minutes, or until the dough is crisp and the toppings are cooked.

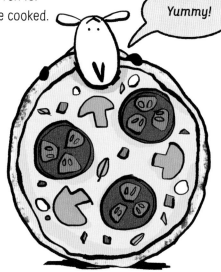

Yummy!

Fun Facts

The Margherita pizza is named after Queen Margherita of Savoy, who chose it as her favourite in 1889.

In the USA, 350 slices of pizza are eaten every second.

The world record for the largest pizza is 37.4m in diameter.

That's a very large pizza!

Cinnamon Buns

Cinnamon buns or rolls or swirls are sweet bread rolls that are served in northern Europe and the USA. Cinnamon is a very popular spice in Sweden. The Swedish town of Gothenburg is famous for the largest cinnamon buns in the world – at over 30cm in diameter.

These rolls are richer than bread dough, because they use milk and butter instead of water.

That's a very large bun!

Dough ingredients

300ml milk
25g butter
15g caster sugar
10g dried yeast
500g strong white flour
1 teaspoon salt

For the filling

150g soft light brown sugar
125g butter, softened
2 tablespoons cinnamon

For the topping

100g icing sugar

You will need a rolling pin and a roasting tin, 24cm x 33cm.

ALLERGIES

Wheat, gluten, dairy

Method

1 Put the milk, butter and sugar in a pan and heat gently until the butter has melted, and the sugar dissolved. Remove from the heat and leave to cool slightly. Once it has become lukewarm or tepid, stir in the yeast.

2 Put the flour and salt in a large mixing bowl. Make a well in the centre of the flour and pour in the milk mixture. Stir the flour into the liquid, until it has been worked into a moist dough.

3 Tip the dough on to the work surface and knead for 10 minutes. Once smooth and elastic, put back in the bowl and cover with oiled cling film to prove until doubled in size.

4 Grease and line the roasting tin. Make your filling by beating together the sugar, cinnamon and butter until smooth.

This needs to be really soft and smooth, so that you can spread it without tearing the dough.

5 Once the dough has proved, knock it back and roll it into a large rectangle approximately 50cm x 25cm. Spread the cinnamon filling completely over the dough. Roll the dough along the long edge into a tight spiral.

To cut the dough, you can use a knife, but a really cool way is to use dental floss! Simply take a 50cm length of floss, wash and dry it, and slide under the dough. Cross the lengths over and pull! The floss slices neatly through the dough!

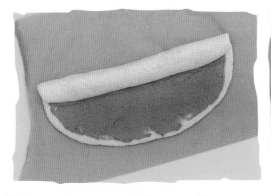

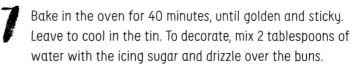

Like this?

6 Cut the roll into 12 equal pieces and arrange in the tin, leaving space for them to increase in size. Leave for 30 minutes covered in lightly oiled cling film. While you wait, heat the oven to 180°C / 400°F or gas mark 6.

7 Bake in the oven for 40 minutes, until golden and sticky. Leave to cool in the tin. To decorate, mix 2 tablespoons of water with the icing sugar and drizzle over the buns.

Cheese and Tomato Stromboli

The stromboli was invented in Philadelpia, USA by Nazzareno Romano in the 1950s.

This recipe is really cool as you can add whatever ingredients you like to the basic cheese and tomato filling. A stromboli is basically a rolled-up pizza that is cut into slices once cooked.

Dough ingredients

10g dried yeast
15g caster sugar
300ml tepid water
500g strong white flour
1 teaspoon salt
1 egg, beaten

For the filling

6 tablespoons tomato sauce
  (see page 86)
Grated mozzarella

You will need a baking tray, a rolling pin, some extra flour for dusting and olive oil.

ALLERGIES

Wheat, gluten, dairy, eggs

Method

1 Add the tepid water to a measuring jug and mix in the yeast and the sugar, until the sugar has dissolved, and the yeast starts to bubble.

2 Put the flour and salt in a large mixing bowl. Make a well in the centre of the flour and pour in the yeast mixture. Stir the flour into the liquid, until it has been worked into a moist dough.

3 Tip the dough on to the work surface and knead for 10 minutes. Once smooth and elastic, put back in the bowl and cover with oiled cling film to prove until doubled in size.

4 Prepare your baking tray by lightly oiling it and then dust with flour.

5 Once the dough has doubled in size, knock it back and roll it into a large rectangle 50cm x 25cm in size.

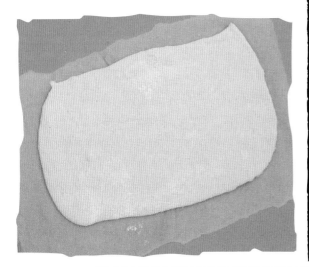

6 Spread the tomato sauce over the dough leaving 2cm uncovered on one of the short edges. Sprinkle over the mozzarella. Brush the uncovered strip with some of the beaten egg.

7 Starting with the short edge that has topping on it, fold the dough over in 10cm folds. Repeat 3–4 times ending with the egg washed strip. Press down the strip firmly to seal.

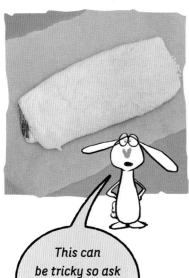

This can be tricky so ask a grown-up to help.

8 Brush all over the stromboli with beaten egg and leave to prove for a further 15 minutes. While you wait, heat the oven to 200°C / 425°F or gas mark 7. Bake in the oven for 30 minutes. Once cooked, leave for 5 minutes before slicing.

This tastes just like pizza! I love it!

Tortillas and Roti

Some breads can be made without yeast and are called flatbreads. These tortilla and roti recipes use flour and oil, as well as water, to make the dough. You still need to knead the dough, but it doesn't have to prove for as long. Both breads are cooked in a hot frying pan.

Tortillas come from Mexico and are very flat. Roti are Indian flatbreads that puff up a little and are eaten with curries.

You should probably ask a grown-up to help you with the cooking!

Tortilla ingredients

250g strong white flour
½ teaspoon salt
2 tablespoons vegetable oil
150ml tepid water

Roti ingredients

115g self-raising flour
115g wholemeal plain flour
1½ teaspoons salt
150ml tepid water
2 tablespoons vegetable oil, plus extra for frying
2 teaspoons unsalted butter, for frying

You will need a rolling pin and a frying pan.

ALLERGIES

Wheat, gluten

Method for both recipes

1 Put the flour (or both flours for roti) and salt in a bowl, and stir together.

This is a much quicker way to make flatbreads...

2 Add the vegetable oil and the water to the bowl, and mix with a spoon, until the dough comes together. You might need to add a little more water, or a little more flour, to the dough so it isn't sticky and forms a ball.

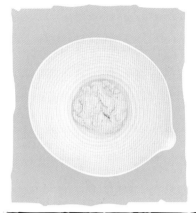 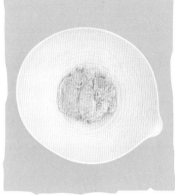

3 Tip the mixture on to a clean work surface, and knead for 5 minutes until smooth and springy. Leave to rest for 30 minutes in a lightly oiled bowl.

Oooh good! Time for a quick pre-bread nap!

4 Once rested, divide the dough into 6 equal pieces. For tortillas, roll each piece into a flat circle about the size of a plate, 20cm in diameter. The roti should be a little thicker, so roll to 12cm in diameter.

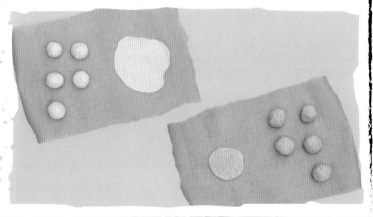

5 If you're making tortillas, heat the frying pan on a high heat and cook the tortillas in the dry pan for 1–2 minutes on both sides until toasted.

In this instance 'dry' means no oil or butter.

6 For roti, heat the frying pan on a high heat and add a little vegetable oil and butter. Once the butter is foaming, add a rolled-out roti to the pan and fry on each side for 2 minutes. When it is golden brown and puffy, remove from the pan and cook the next one. Wrap in foil to keep warm in the oven.

CORE BAKING SKILL
#8 Dairy-free and Gluten-free Baking

Some people find that dairy foods or foods containing gluten make them feel unwell, but there are lots of delicious recipes that don't contain butter, milk or flour. This lemon meringue roulade is perfect for people who can't eat gluten. The egg whites and sugar are whisked into a pillowy meringue.

We fill the meringue with lemon curd and whipped cream – I can't wait!

Lemon Meringue Roulade

Meringue ingredients

5 eggs
200g caster sugar
50g flaked almonds

For the filling

300ml double cream

6 tablespoons lemon curd
Icing sugar for dusting

You will need a Swiss roll tin or baking tray, 33 x 24cm.

ALLERGIES

Dairy, eggs, nuts

A Swiss roll tin is slightly deeper than a normal baking tray with sides about 3cm high. Most baking tins will work though, if they are the right dimensions.

Make sure you don't get any egg yolk in the egg whites, or they won't whisk properly.

Method

1 Heat the oven to 180°C / 400°F or gas mark 6. Line your Swiss roll tin leaving at least 5cm of paper over the edge of the tin.

2 Separate the eggs into whites and yolks. Put the whites into a large, clean mixing bowl, and put the yolks to one side for another recipe. (See page 109 for instructions.)

3 Using a hand whisk, beat the egg whites until they form soft peaks. This could take a few minutes and use a lot of energy! You'll know they are ready when you lift up your whisk and the white foam doesn't drop off.

If you have an electric whisk you can use that instead, but make sure a grown up is nearby.

4 Gradually add the caster sugar to the egg whites until it is all used up and the meringue is thick and glossy.

It's supposed to stay in the bowl!

5 Tip the meringue onto the Swiss roll tin, and spread it out to all the corners. Sprinkle with the flaked almonds.

6 Bake in the oven for 10 minutes, and then turn the oven down to 160°C / 320°F or gas mark 3 for another 15 minutes.

Ask a grown-up to help you with the next step!

7 Take a large sheet of baking parchment, bigger than the meringue, and place it on top of the tin. Carefully flip the tin over so the nut-covered side is face down. Slowly peel off the parchment lining and leave to cool for about 10 minutes.

8 Whip the cream until it is doubled in volume, then spread on top of the meringue. Take the lemon curd and spread gently on top of the cream. Using the baking parchment to help you, take the long edge and start to roll it up as tightly as you can.

9 Place on a board or plate with the join on the bottom, and sieve over icing sugar to decorate.

This cake should stay in the fridge if you don't eat it immediately.

How is that even possible?

Dairy-free Banana, Date and Walnut Bread

This yummy banana bread uses really ripe bananas – even the ones that have gone black – to make it moist and sticky! The walnuts are lovely and crunchy, and the dates add an amazing toffee-like flavour.

Bread ingredients

3 large, very ripe bananas

75ml vegetable oil, plus extra for greasing

100g light soft brown sugar

225g self-raising flour

2 teaspoons baking powder

50g walnuts, chopped

50g dates, chopped

You will need a loaf tin.

ALLERGIES

Wheat, gluten, nuts

If your dates have stones in, be sure to remove them before chopping!

Method

1 Heat the oven to 180°C / 400°F or gas mark 6. Grease and line a loaf tin.

2 Mash the bananas with a fork and add them to a large mixing bowl.

3 Add the vegetable oil and sugar, and mix well.

4 Add the flour and baking powder, and stir again until all the flour is combined. Finally, add the chopped walnuts and dates.

Fun Facts

Dates grow on the date palm tree.

Date pits are the stones in the middle of the fruits.

A 2000-year-old pit has recently sprouted leaves in a laboratory.

5 Pour into the tin and flatten the top of the cake mix.

You might need to cover the top of the cake in foil to stop it burning.

6 Bake in the oven for 40 minutes. Check halfway through to see if the cake is browning.

Use your oven gloves to wrap the foil around the cake!

7 Remove from the oven and check to see if it is cooked with a skewer. Leave to cool in the tin.

I like butter on my banana bread!

Dairy-free Carrot Cake

Carrot cake first appeared in the Middle Ages when carrots were used to sweeten puddings, instead of expensive sugar. In 1814, a French recipe from King Louis XVI's former chef describes a 'Gâteau de Carottes', and carrot cake became popular again in the UK during World War II, when sugar was rationed.

Spices—

Uh uh! This is my page! Spices and dried fruit are also added to make a delicious teatime treat!

Cake ingredients

175g light soft brown sugar
175ml vegetable oil
3 eggs
3 medium carrots
100g raisins
1 orange, zested
175g self-raising flour
1 teaspoon bicarbonate of soda
1 teaspoon cinnamon
½ teaspoon grated nutmeg

For the icing

175g icing sugar
2 tablespoons orange juice

Makes 9 squares

You will need a square brownie tin, 23cm x 23cm.

ALLERGIES
Wheat, gluten, eggs

Carrot cake is my favourite!

Fun Facts

Carrots are root vegetables.

Carrots do help you to see in the dark!

Carrots haven't always been orange. Dutch carrot growers invented the orange carrot to honour the Dutch Royal Family, the House of Orange.

Method

1 Heat the oven to 160°C / 350°F or gas mark 4. Grease and line the brownie tin, including the sides.

2 Add the sugar, vegetable oil and eggs to a large mixing bowl and whisk together.

3 Peel and grate the carrots on the large hole side of a grater. Add to the mixture, along with the raisins and orange zest.

Mind your fingers!

4 Sieve the flour, bicarbonate of soda and spices into the bowl. Mix together and add to the brownie tin.

5 Bake in the oven for 40–45 minutes, until the cake feels firm and springy in the middle.

6 Cool in the tin for 5 minutes, then turn out onto a wire rack. When completely cool, mix the orange juice and icing sugar to make the icing. Drizzle over the cake.

Mmmmm – delicious!

Gluten-free Lemon and Almond Polenta Cake

This delicious flour-free lemon cake uses ground almonds and polenta instead of flour. It has a nutty texture and is denser than a normal sponge cake, but soaks up the lemon drizzle beautifully.

Polenta is made from ground maize and is known as 'maize flour' or 'cornmeal'.

Cake ingredients

140g butter, softened
250g caster sugar
3 eggs
2 lemons, zest and juice
200g ground almonds
175g polenta or fine cornmeal
1 teaspoon baking powder

For the drizzle

140g caster sugar
1 lemon, juiced

You will need a brownie tin, 23cm x 23cm.

ALLERGIES

Dairy, eggs

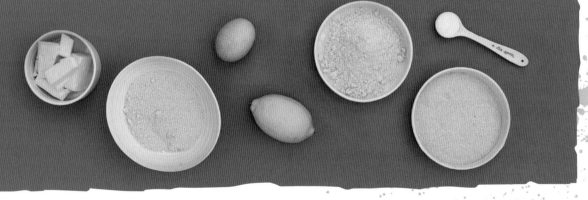

Method

1 Heat the oven to 150°C / 325°F or gas mark 3. Grease and line the cake tin, including the sides.

2 Cream the butter and sugar together until light and fluffy. Add the eggs one at a time until all mixed in. Add the lemon juice and zest.

3 Add the ground almonds, polenta and baking powder and stir well. Tip the mixture into the brownie tin, and smooth the top. Bake in the oven for 40 minutes.

4 The cake is ready when it is golden in colour and has come away from the sides of the tin. Remove from the oven and prick holes in the cake. Mix the sugar and lemon juice.

5 Pour the drizzle over the cake and let it soak in. Allow the cake to cool completely before eating.

Even I can't get this one wrong!

Oh, really...

Dairy-free and Gluten-free Coconut Macaroons

I can hear a horse! Clipetty clop, clip clop!

Using only four ingredients, these coconut macaroons are really easy to make! They're soft and chewy on the inside, and crisp and golden on the outside.

Macaroon ingredients

2 egg whites (see page 109 for instructions)
100g caster sugar
30g ground almonds
250g desiccated coconut

You will need a baking tray.

ALLERGIES

Eggs, nuts

Fun Facts

Coconuts are tropical fruits.

Every part of the coconut has a use.

The fruit was called 'coco' (grinning face) by 16th-century Portuguese sailors because they thought the three holes on its shell looked like a smiling face.

Method

1 Heat the oven to 150°C / 325°F or gas mark 3. Grease and line the baking tray.

2 Whisk the egg whites until they form soft peaks. Gradually add the sugar, a spoonful at a time, until the peaks are shiny.

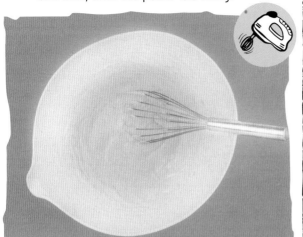

3 Fold in the ground almonds and coconut. The mixture should hold together in clumps.

4 Using 2 teaspoons, make ping-pong-ball-sized mounds of mixture on the baking tray.

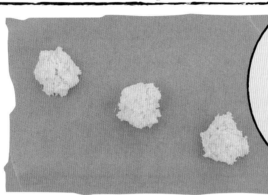

I prefer my macaroons in a ball shape, as they are more chewy in the middle, but you can flatten them if you like.

5 Bake in the oven for 20 minutes until they just start to turn golden. Leave to cool on a wire rack.

Mewwy mmmph melicious...

What did you say?

I said... chewy and delicious!

Dairy-free Spiced Fruit Cake

Fruit cakes date back to Roman times, when Roman soldiers used them as long-lasting, portable meals. The Middle Ages saw spices added, as well as honey. The Victorians added sherry.

This rich fruit cake doesn't contain any butter, but has lots of different types of dried fruit and would be perfect decorated as a Christmas cake.

Traditionally, Christmas Cakes are covered in marzipan and royal icing.

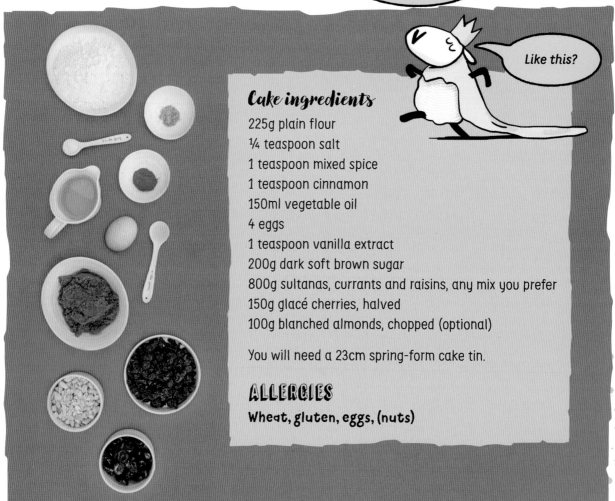

Like this?

Cake ingredients

225g plain flour
¼ teaspoon salt
1 teaspoon mixed spice
1 teaspoon cinnamon
150ml vegetable oil
4 eggs
1 teaspoon vanilla extract
200g dark soft brown sugar
800g sultanas, currants and raisins, any mix you prefer
150g glacé cherries, halved
100g blanched almonds, chopped (optional)

You will need a 23cm spring-form cake tin.

ALLERGIES
Wheat, gluten, eggs, (nuts)

Method

1 Heat the oven to 120°C / 275°F or gas mark 1. Grease and line the cake tin.

For cakes that bake for a long time, it's best to double line the tin. See page 108 for instructions.

2 In a large bowl, add the flour, salt and spices and stir. In another bowl, mix the eggs, vegetable oil, vanilla extract and sugar, and whisk until light and fluffy.

3 Tip the egg mixture into the flour bowl and mix. Add all the fruit and nuts, and mix well.

4 Tip the cake mix into the cake tin and smooth out the surface. Bake in the oven for 2 hours and 30 minutes, or until a skewer comes out clean. You might need to cover with foil halfway through.

5 Remove from the oven and leave in the tin to cool.

It's absolutely delicious to eat just like this, but if you want to make it extra special, you can ice it too!

Marzipanning the cake

400g marzipan
4 tablespoons apricot jam

ALLERGIES

Eggs, nuts

Marzipan is a paste made from almonds, sugar and egg whites, and is often used to make sweets.

Method

1 Dust your work surface with icing sugar. Soften the marzipan in your hands. Cut the block in half. Form one half into a ball and roll out in a circle to cover the top of the cake. Use your cake tin as a guide.

2 Use the other half to roll out a rectangle, 40cm x 30cm. Cut the marzipan in half parallel to the long side so you have have two 40cm x 15cm strips, to cover the sides of the cake.

If you measure the height of the cake, you can cut the strips so that they jut up slightly. Then the top will fit nicely in the space left.

3 Warm the apricot jam in the microwave and brush it all over the cake. Carefully stick the strips of marzipan around the cake joining the edges together. You may need to trim the side pieces to fit. Then place the marzipan circle on top of the cake.

4 Cover with a clean tea towel and leave the cake for a day in a cool place to dry.

Royal Icing

For the icing

500g royal icing sugar
Cake decorations

Method

1 Place 75ml of water in a mixing bowl. Sieve the royal icing sugar into the bowl and mix with a wooden spoon until thick like a paste. This icing hardens quickly so keep the bowl covered with a damp tea towel.

2 Spread the icing over the cake, top and sides. If you want a flat finish, you can use a clean ruler to spread the icing evenly. Or use a fork to create a snowy scene.

3 Decorate with stars or holly leaves to create a festive atmosphere.

Why do we have to wait until Christmas? I think it should be called Tuesday cake.

Baking Techniques

Greasing and lining tins and trays

Round tins

To cut out a circle of baking parchment:

- Tear off a rectangle with the short side slightly wider than the cake tin.

- Fold the rectangle in half.

- Fold it in half twice more and then diagonally.

- Hold the pointed corner over the centre of the cake tin and cut an arc following the circumference of the cake tin.

- Unfold the shape and you will have a rough circle of baking parchment to line your tin base.

Use the remaining bits of parchment to grease the tins with butter, before lining, so the lining paper sticks to the bottom and sides.

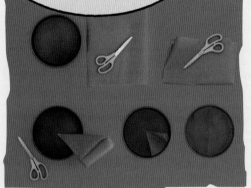

Loaf tins and brownie tins

Tear off a piece of baking parchment 1½ times longer than the length of the tin.

Grease the tin with butter and place the middle of the parchment over the tin. Press down and fold the excess paper over the edges.

To line a brownie tin, cut the greaseproof paper to 30cm x 30cm. Grease with butter, push down into the tin and smooth out the corners.

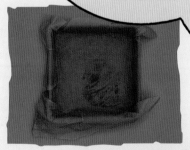

Double lining cake tins

Some cakes – like the spicy fruit cake on page 104 – need double lining. Double up the base, using butter or oil to stick them down. For the sides, use the cake tin to work out how long the greaseproof paper needs to be, tear it off and then fold in half. Fit the folded edge to the bottom of the cake tin.

Taking cakes out of their tins

If you've greased and lined the tins properly, cakes are normally easy to get out of their tins. Sometimes, you might need a little help. Always run a round-bladed knife around the sides of the tin before trying to lift your cake out.

Loose-bottom tin

Stand the cake tin on top of a tin of baked beans and gently ease the tin down. This means you can easily slide the cake slice between the tin base and the cake to lift it off.

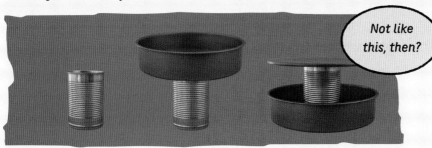

Not like this, then?

Separating eggs

It's important to remember to go slowly and carefully. If even a tiny bit of yolk gets into the egg whites, they won't whisk properly.

Once you've learnt how to separate an egg into its white (the clear liquid bit) and its yolk (the yellow circle), there are all sorts of recipes you can make.

1. Getting your hands dirty

Over a bowl, crack the egg on the side of the bowl or with a knife. Use your hand to scoop up the egg, and let the egg white dribble through.

With clean hands obviously!

2. Using a slotted spoon

Place the spoon in a bowl. Crack the egg into it. Let the white run through and off the spoon and lift the yolk clear.

It's no yolk, I'm not very good at this.

Piping icing

1. Put the nozzle into the piping bag and push until it is poking out of the end of the bag.

2. Put the bag, nozzle down, into a glass and ask a grown-up to hold it for you.

3. Spoon the icing into the bag. Use an elastic band to tie the top of the bag.

4. Pick up the bag, take hold of the top and grasp it in your fist. Slowly twist the bag so that the icing squeezes down towards the nozzle.

5. Practise on a plate first. From the top, gently squeeze out some icing in a swirl and release when you get to the centre. Or keep squeezing, holding the nozzle low down and pull up to release the final peak.

Ooops!

Melting chocolate

You can use a microwave, but it can be easier to see how quickly the chocolate is melting if you use a bain-marie.

Bain-marie literally means 'Mary's bath' in French and is attributed to an ancient alchemist, or scientist, called Mary. Another name is a 'double boiler'.

1. Take a heat-proof bowl and rest it on top of a small pan of water. Make sure that the water doesn't touch the bowl.

3. Heat the water to a gentle simmer. Simmering means you see tiny bubbles, rather than large angry bubbles which means it is boiling.

4. Place the chocolate in the bowl. As the chocolate begins to melt, you can gently push the pieces around.

Use your oven gloves to take the bowl off the pan, and make sure you turn the heat off first.

Making chocolate curls

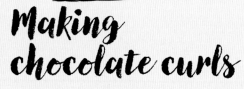

Method 1. Use the coarse side of a grater and grate the chocolate.

Method 2. Take a vegetable peeler, and as if you were peeling a carrot, pull it down the edge of the chocolate.

Method 3. SUPER ADVANCED – Place the chocolate bar vertically on a wooden board in front of you. Take a sharp knife in both hands, one holding the tip and one the handle and hold at 45°. Pull the knife across the chocolate bar towards you to make the curls.

Use chocolate that's been taken out of the fridge for 10 minutes first.

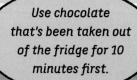

It's best to have a grown-up with you when you do this!

Hey, that's my line!

Index

Acknowledgements

With thanks to Emily – daughter of Mr Griff, illustrator extraordinaire – for
her input, Mr Griff himself, Tina, the wondrous photographer, the various
Noodle Juice family members who put up with the ceaseless baking and
photo shoots in mid-summer heat, and last, but not least, the mixing bowl!

(Only washed approximately 250 times in two weeks!)